MCDOUGAL, LITTELL
Spelling

Dolores Boylston Bohen
Assistant Superintendent
Fairfax County Public Schools
Fairfax County, Virginia

Joyce Moore
Primary Teacher
Fairfax County, Virginia

2
PLUM LEVEL

Houghton Mifflin Company   Boston
Atlanta   Dallas   Geneva, Illinois   Palo Alto   Princeton

recycled paper

Objectives

- to teach the spelling of **words** as well as the spelling of sounds
- to stress the recognition of **structural** similarities as well as phonetic similarities
- to strengthen **associative** and **visual memory**
- to reinforce the **three modes of learning:** visual, auditory, and kinesthetic

Organization

Each lesson presents a word list that demonstrates one spelling pattern or generalization. The list is followed by three types of activities:

Practice the Words—three activities that require students to examine and write the words on the spelling list

Build Word Power—an activity that extends the application of words on the spelling list in a broader language arts context

Reach Out for New Words—two activities in which students work with new words that follow the spelling pattern

CONSULTANTS FOR THIS TEXT

Stuart Cunningham, Principal, Irvine Unified School District, Irvine, California
Jan Dagher, Teacher, Portage Public Schools, Portage, Michigan
Ina Lu Francis, Teacher, Conroe Independent School District, Conroe, Texas
Helene Hoffman, Teacher, Jefferson Public Schools, Jefferson, Wisconsin
David Johnson, Curriculum Specialist, Mount Diablo School District, Concord, California
Elaine Rappel, Teacher, School District of Chetek, Chetek, Wisconsin
Susan Vittone, Teacher, District 208, Oneida, Illinois
Doris Watkins, Teacher, Durham County Schools, Durham, North Carolina
Patricia Gomez Wiltshire, Bilingual Teacher, Detroit Public Schools, Detroit, Michigan
Elsa Woods, Principal, Durham County Schools, Durham, North Carolina

ISBN 0–8123–8576–4

Copyright © 1994 by McDougal, Littell & Company
Box 1667, Evanston, Illinois 60204
All rights reserved. Printed in the United States of America.

12 13 14 15 -WC-02 01

Contents

How to Spell a Word

1. Look at the word.

2. Say the word.

3. Spell the word aloud.

4. Copy the word.

5. Picture the word in your mind.

6. Cover the word and write it.

   Check for mistakes.
   If you have made a mistake,
   repeat steps 1 to 6.

a b c d e f g h i j k l m n

o p q r s t u v w x y z

A B C D E F G H I J

K L M N O P Q R S

T U V W X Y Z

a b c d e f g h i j
k l m n o p q r
s t u v w x y z
A B C D E F G H I
J K L M N O P Q R
S T U V W X Y Z

it   has   as   not

us   job   if   yes

him   red   up   run

The letters **a, e, i, o, u** are <u>vowels</u>. The vowel sound in each spelling word is called a <u>short</u> <u>vowel</u> sound.

Practice the Words

A Write the spelling words that go with each vowel.

a   **i**   **u**

_____   _____   _____

_____   _____   _____

_____   _____   _____

e   **o**

_____   _____

_____   _____

B Write the spelling words that go in the sentences.

1. Bob ran __up__ the hill.

2. What time is __i_____?

3. She __h_____ a new hat.

4. We may __n_____ go.

5. Mom has a __j_____ in a shop.

6. Come with __u_____.

C Add vowels to make spelling words.

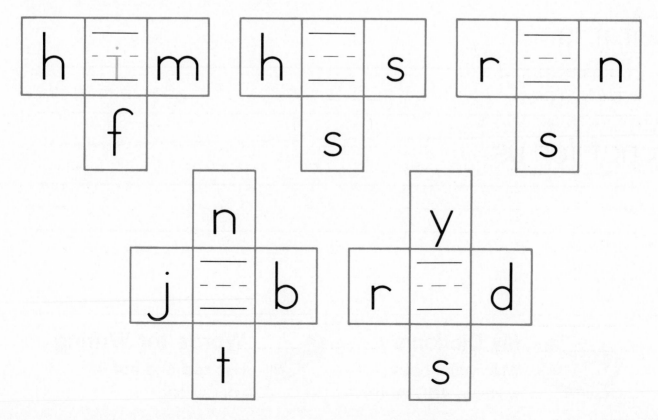

Build Word Power

Writing

Write a sentence with each word group.

1. **as red as**

_____

- - - - - - - - - - - - - - - - - -

_____

2. **give him a**

_____

- - - - - - - - - - - - - - - - - -

_____

3. **has a job**

_____

- - - - - - - - - - - - - - - - - -

_____

4. **if it is**

_____

- - - - - - - - - - - - - - - - - -

_____

5. **not for us**

_____

- - - - - - - - - - - - - - - - - -

_____

My Dictionary
Write your spelling
words in **ABC** order.

Words for Writing
Use **red** and **not** in
your writing.

Reach Out for New Words

A Add the missing vowels to make new words.

1. __ pon

2. g __ ve

3. n __ xt

4. __ fter

5. w __ nt

6. pl __ s

B Write the new words that go in the story.

Once __u__ a time there was a

boy who wanted a pet. Day __a__

day he __w__ to the pet store.

The store owner said, "I'll __g__

you a dog __p__ some fish." The

__n__ day the boy took his pets home!

gave	grade	came	note
made	twice	pie	side
these	broke	blue	date

The first vowel in each spelling word is a long vowel.
You do not hear the final **e** in each word. It is silent.

Practice the Words

A Write the spelling words. Circle the first vowel in each word.
Draw a line through the silent **e**.

1. gave
2. ________
3. ________
4. ________
5. ________
6. ________
7. ________
8. ________
9. ________
10. ________
11. ________
12. ________

B Write the spelling words that go with each vowel.

a

e

o

i

u

C Add vowels to make spelling words.

g _ v _
r
d _ t _

t w _ c _
h
s
m

blue	gave	pie	came	note	made
twice	grade	date	side	these	broke

Build Word Power

Circle the word in each line that is spelled correctly.

1. dayt   (date)   dat

2. came   caim   caem

3. grayd   graid   grade

4. syd   side   sied

5. brok   broak   broke

6. blue   bloo   bluw

7. theez   thees   these

8. py   pie   pye

9. noat   note   noot

10. twice   twise   twyce

My Dictionary
Write your spelling
words in **ABC** order.

Words for Writing
Use **made** and **blue** in
your writing.

Reach Out for New Words

A Add the missing vowels to make new words.

1. l ⁼ te

2. g ⁼ te

3. sunsh ⁼ ne

4. cost ⁼ me

5. sp ⁼ ke

6. par ⁼ de

B Write the new words that go in the story.

It was a day filled with ___s___.

Mom ___s___ to me. She said, "Today

you march in the big ___p___!

Put on your ___c___. Hurry so you

are not ___l___."

mak~~e~~ + ing	=	making		rul~~e~~ + ing	=	ruling
hop~~e~~ + ing	=	hoping		jok~~e~~ + ing	=	joking
hid~~e~~ + ing	=	hiding		div~~e~~ + ing	=	diving
bik~~e~~ + ing	=	biking		bak~~e~~ + ing	=	baking
nam~~e~~ + ing	=	naming		rop~~e~~ + ing	=	roping
rac~~e~~ + ing	=	racing		us~~e~~ + ing	=	using

When a word ends with silent **e**, drop the **e** before you add **ing**.

Practice the Words

A Add **ing** to each word to make the spelling words.
Cross out the **e** before you add **ing**.

1. make ~~ing~~ _____
2. joke _____
3. name _____
4. hope _____
5. bike _____
6. rope _____
7. dive _____
8. race _____
9. rule _____
10. hide _____
11. bake _____
12. use _____

16

B Add **ing** to each word. Write the **ing** word that goes in each sentence.

hope	bake	hide	name	use	dive

1. Sam is _baking_ a cake.

2. Ann is _____ under the bed.

3. He is _____ to win a prize.

4. What are you _____ the cat?

5. The girl is _____ into the lake.

6. We are _____ the red paint.

C Write each word with the **ing** ending.

1. rule _ruling_

2. make _____

3. joke _____

4. bike _____

5. rope _____

6. race _____

Write each spelling word without the **ing** ending.

1. roping ___rope___   7. naming _____

2. making _____   8. diving _____

3. hiding _____   9. ruling _____

4. biking _____   10. hoping _____

5. joking _____   11. baking _____

6. using _____   12. racing _____

 **My Dictionary**
Write your spelling
words in **ABC** order.

 Words for Writing
Use **making** and **using** in
your writing.

like　　bite　　time　　close　　rake　　vote

Reach Out for New Words

A Add **ing** to each word. Write the new **ing** words.

1. _____

2. _____

3. _____

4. _____

5. _____

6. _____

B Circle the correct spelling of each **ing** word.

1. bite　　(biting)　　biteing

2. time　　timeing　　timing

3. like　　likeing　　liking

4. close　　closing　　closeing

5. rake　　rakeing　　raking

6. vote　　voting　　voteing

cry   may   any

by   way   only

shy   gray   many

sky   today   very

Practice the Words

A Write the spelling words. Circle the **y** in each word.

1. _____ 5. _____ 9. _____

2. _____ 6. _____ 10. _____

3. _____ 7. _____ 11. _____

4. _____ 8. _____ 12. _____

B Write the spelling words that go in the sentences.

1. The ___s___ is blue.

2. Dad says I ___m___ come.

3. The little mouse is ___g___.

4. My birthday is ___t___.

5. Be home ___b___ noon.

6. Which ___w___ did they go?

C Find letters that fit in the shapes to make spelling words.

1.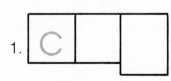

2.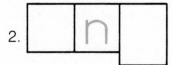

3.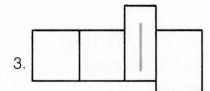

4.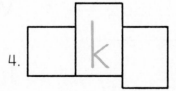

5.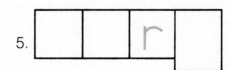

6.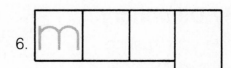

Dictionary

Dictionary words are in ABC order.
Words beginning with **a** come first.
Words beginning with **b** come next.
Words beginning with **c** come after **b**.

This is called <u>alphabetical</u> <u>order</u>.

a̲nd

b̲ed

c̲an

a b c d e f g h i j k l m n o p q r s t u v w x y z

Write each list of spelling words in alphabetical order.

List 1

any   1. any

cry   2. _____

gray   3. _____

by   4. _____

shy   5. _____

List 2

only   1. many

way   2. _____

very   3. _____

today   4. _____

many   5. _____

 **My Dictionary**
Write your spelling
words in **ABC** order.

 Words for Writing
Use **sky** and **today** in
your writing.

ready   clay   pry   jelly   pretty   sly   hay

Reach Out for New Words

A Find the word in each line that ends with **y**.
Circle the word. Then write the word.

1.	r	e	a	d	y	w
2.	s	o	c	l	a	y
3.	u	p	r	y	o	u
4.	j	e	l	l	y	w
5.	p	r	e	t	t	y
6.	o	n	s	l	y	v
7.	q	r	h	a	y	l

1. _ready_

2. _____

3. _____

4. _____

5. _____

6. _____

7. _____

B Write new words that fit the clues.

1. all set to start

2. pull a lid off

3. use this to make things

4. eat this with peanut butter

book	look	hood	stood
good	cook	took	foot
brook	wool	hook	wood

Practice the Words

A Write the spelling words. Circle the **oo** in each word.

1. book

2. _____

3. _____

4. _____

5. _____

6. _____

7. _____

8. _____

9. _____

10. _____

11. _____

12. _____

24

B Write the **oo** words for the pictures.

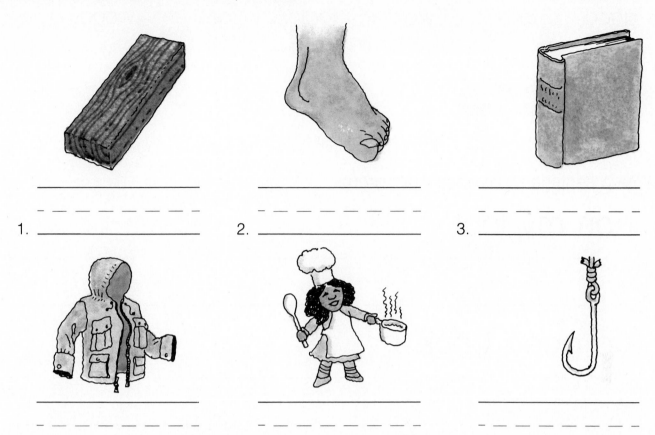

1. _____

2. _____

3. _____

4. _____

5. _____

6. _____

C Write the **oo** words that go in the sentences.

1. This ice cream tastes _g_____.

2. Joe _st_____ in line.

3. Dad _t_____ us to the store.

4. Did you _l_____ at the map?

5. We get _w_____ from sheep.

6. Fish swim in the _br_____.

Build Word Power

Writing

Write a sentence with each word group.

1. on my foot

----

2. a good book

----

3. in the brook

----

4. stood by me

----

5. took a look

 **My Dictionary**
Write your spelling
words in **ABC** order.

 Words for Writing
Use **book** and **good** in
your writing.

26

shook   cookie   hoof   goodbye   woods

Reach Out for New Words

A Follow the directions to make new **oo** words.

1. Put **s** before **hook**.

_____

2. Change the **k** in **hook** to **f**.

_____

3. Change the **h** in **hood** to **w**.
   Add **s** at the end.

_____

4. Change the **f** in **food** to **g**.
   Add **bye** at the end.

_____

5. Change the **t** in **took** to **c**.
   Add **ie** at the end.

_____

B Write the new **oo** words that go in the sentences.

1. The pony hurt one _____.

2. We all waved _____.

3. She _____ my hand.

4. Let's walk in the _____.

5. May I have a _____?

27

boot   pool   noon   zoo

fool   room   tooth   food

school   loose   moon   too

Practice the Words

A Write the spelling words. Circle the **oo** in each word.

1. _____   5. _____   9. _____

2. _____   6. _____   10. _____

3. _____   7. _____   11. _____

4. _____   8. _____   12. _____

B Make the word groups into sentences. Start each sentence with a capital letter. End each sentence with a period. Circle the **oo** words.

1. pool boot My fell in the

2. food noon eat at We

3. tooth My loose is

Dictionary

C Write the two lists of words in alphabetical order. The first word in each list is done for you.

boot   1. boot   room   1. noon

loose 2.   zoo   2.

food   3.   noon   3.

moon   4.   tooth 4.

too   5.   school 5.

boot	pool	noon	zoo	moon	school
fool	room	tooth	food	too	loose

Build Word Power

Find and circle eight **oo** words. Look across and down. Write the words.

b	o	o	t	x	u
l	z	r	o	o	m
m	r	z	o	o	p
o	l	o	o	s	e
o	q	p	o	o	l
n	o	o	n	n	r

1. _____

2. _____

3. _____

4. _____

5. _____

6. _____

7. _____

8. _____

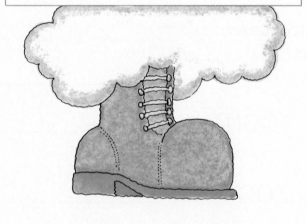

My Dictionary
Write your spelling words in **ABC** order.

Words for Writing
Use **school** and **zoo** in your writing.

Reach Out for New Words

A Write the new **oo** words for the pictures.

1. _____

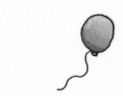

2. _____

3. _____

4. _____

5. _____

6. _____

B Write the new **oo** words that fit the clues.

1. You can sit on this.

_____

2. It is a very large animal.

_____

3. To pick out a thing.

_____

4. You stir with this.

_____

5. You sweep the floor with this.

_____

31

bang   ring   hang
king   long   sing
wing   bring   song
swing   spring   strong

Practice the Words

A Write the spelling words. Circle the **ng** in each word.

1. _____

2. _____

3. _____

4. _____

5. _____

6. _____

7. _____

8. _____

9. _____

10. _____

11. _____

12. _____

B Write the spelling words that go in the sentences.

1. The bird hurt its _____.

2. The _____ wears a crown.

3. David sang a _____.

4. We have a _____ way to go.

5. Flowers grow in the _____.

6. You must be _____ to lift that.

C Write each spelling word with the **ing** ending.

1. bang   banging

2. swing   _____

3. bring   _____

4. sing   _____

5. hang   _____

6. ring   _____

| bang | wing | ring | bring | hang | song |
| king | swing | long | spring | sing | strong |

Build Word Power

Dictionary

Dictionary words are in alphabetical order. Many words begin with the same letter. When this happens, the <u>second</u> letter is used to put the words in alphabetical order.

r**a**ce

r**o**pe

r**u**le

a b c d e f g h i j k l m n o p q r s t u v w x y z

Five spelling words begin with the same letter.

What is that letter? _____

Look at the second letter in each word. Write the five words in alphabetical order.

1. _____   4. _____

2. _____   5. _____

3. _____

My Dictionary
Write your spelling words in **ABC** order.

Words for Writing
Use **bang** and **ring** in your writing.

34

Reach Out for New Words

A Follow the directions to make new **ng** words.

1. Change the **k** in **king** to **cl**.

2. Change the **i** in **sing** to **a**.

3. Change the **h** in **hang** to **r**.

4. Change the **w** in **wing** to **st**.

5. Put **st** in front of **ring**.

B Write new **ng** words that go in the sentences.

1. Tie the box with _____.

2. The school bell _____.

3. A baby will _____ to its mother.

4. That bee may _____ you.

5. We _____ a new song today.

run   hiding   strong

pie   many   cry

note   school   red

biking moon   making

today   bring   stood

Practice

A Write the spelling words for the pictures.

1. _____   2. _____   3. _____

4. _____   5. _____   6. _____

B Write the spelling words that go in the sentences.

1. Do we go to school _____?

2. There are _____ children here.

3. The _____ is in the sky.

4. What are you _____ with clay?

5. The _____ girl lifted the big box.

6. Can you write a _____ for me?

C Write each silent **e** word with the **ing** ending.

1. hide _____

2. note _____

3. bike _____

4. make _____

D Write the words that rhyme with the clues and fit in the shapes.

1. gray

2. shy

3. penny

Proofreading

A Cross out the spelling mistake in each sentence. Write each sentence correctly.

1. The mune is bright.

2. I like apple pye.

3. She stoud over there.

4. Did you bringg the ball?

38

Dictionary

B Write each list of words in alphabetical order.

1

bring _____

cry _____

bike _____

2

note _____

hiding _____

many _____

3

pie _____

today _____

strong _____

C Write the spelling word that rhymes with each word.

1. hiking _____

2. fun _____

3. fool _____

4. sing _____

5. baking _____

6. wood _____

7. bed _____

8. away _____

one	four	seven	ten
two	five	eight	eleven
three	six	nine	twelve

Spell the Words

A Write the spelling word that matches each numeral.

1 _____

6 _____

10 _____

5 _____

3 _____

9 _____

2 _____

8 _____

11 _____

4 _____

7 _____

12 _____

B Count the number of things in each picture. Write the
correct number word for each picture.

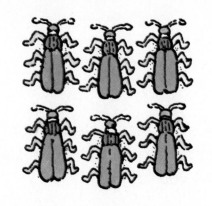

1. _____

2. _____

3. _____

4. _____

5. _____

6. _____

C Write the number words that answer the questions.

_____

1. What is two + one?

_____

2. What is three + six?

_____

3. What is ten − two?

_____

4. What is twelve − eleven?

Write With the Words

Write the spelling word in the story that matches each numeral. Then write your own ending for the story. Use as many of the spelling words as you can. What do you think happened next?

Our class was keeping (12) _____ frogs in a tank. One day, the frogs were gone!

"I see (1) _____ hopping on the table," yelled Mike. "That leaves (11) _____."

"There are (3) _____ on the floor," called Jeanne. "We must still find _____."

_____

My Dictionary
Write your spelling words in **ABC** order.

Words for Writing
Use **two** and **four** in your writing.

42

Number words can tell place in the line.

1 2 3 4 5 6 7 8 9 10 11 12

A Write the number words in counting order.

second	ninth	fourth	tenth	seventh	eleventh
fifth	first	sixth	eighth	third	twelfth

1. first

2. _____

3. _____

4. _____

5. _____

6. _____

7. _____

8. _____

9. _____

10. _____

11. _____

12. _____

B Look at the s.
Color the first, third, fifth, and sixth s.

43

aim   nail   rain   mail
sail   wait   praise   paint
trail   plain   paid   tail

Practice the Words

A Write the spelling words. Circle the **ai** in each word.

1. aim   5. _____   9. _____

2. _____   6. _____   10. _____

3. _____   7. _____   11. _____

4. _____   8. _____   12. _____

B Write the **ai** words for the pictures.

1. _____

2. _____

3. _____

4. _____

5. _____

6. _____

C Write the **ai** words that go in the sentences.

1. We will __w_____ in line.

2. You should __pr_____ his hard work.

3. Maria walked along the __tr_____.

4. Did you __a____ at the target?

5. He __p_____ for the bike.

6. My shoes are very __pi_____.

Build Word Power

Proofreading

Cross out the spelling mistakes in the sentences.
Write each sentence correctly.

1. I went to ~~male~~ a letter.

2. Fred pade for a nale.

3. I can paynt a picture.

4. How long did you wate?

My Dictionary
Write your spelling
words in **ABC** order.

Words for Writing
Use **nail** and **paint** in
your writing.

Reach Out for New Words

A Find new **ai** words. Circle them. Then write the words on the lines.

1.	s	n	a	i	l	e
2.	o	t	r	a	i	n
3.	s	t	l	a	i	d
4.	i	b	r	a	i	n
5.	c	h	a	i	n	w
6.	k	m	a	i	n	u

1. _____

2. _____

3. _____

4. _____

5. _____

6. _____

B Write the new **ai** words that rhyme with these words.

rain _____   _____

paid _____ trail _____

47

car   yard   start   park

hard   art   mark   far

large   sharp   barn   farm

Add **s** to make a word mean more than one.

one car 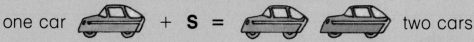 + **S** = two cars

When **s** is added, the word is called <u>plural</u>.

Practice the Words

A Write the spelling words. Circle the **ar** in each word.

1. car

2. ___

3. ___

4. ___

5. ___

6. ___

7. ___

8. ___

9. ___

10. ___

11. ___

12. ___

48

B Add **s** to make the spelling words plural.
Write the words.

1. car   +s   two _____

2. farm   +s   two _____

3. yard   +s   two _____

4. park   +s   two _____

5. barn   +s   two _____

6. mark   +s   two _____

C Write the spelling words that help to tell the story.
Add **s** if the word means more than one.

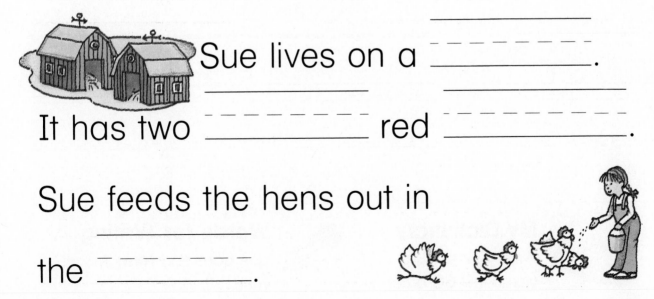

Sue lives on a _____.

It has two _____ red _____.

Sue feeds the hens out in

the _____.

yard   art   car   hard   sharp   start
barn   far   large   park   farm   mark

Build Word Power

Dictionary

There are two words at the top of each page in the dictionary. They are called <u>guide words</u>. The guide word on the left tells you the first word on the page. The guide word on the right tells you the last word on the page. The words on the page are in <u>alphabetical order</u>.

a b c d e f g h i j k l m n o p q r s t u v w x y z

Look at each pair of guide words. What spelling words go with each pair of guide words? Write the words in alphabetical order. For some words you will have to look at the second or third letter. The first set is done for you.

apple	clown	face	hope	lamp	pen
art					
barn					
car					

My Dictionary
Write your spelling words in **ABC** order.

Words for Writing
Use **barn** and **farm** in your writing.

50

card   target   carpet   partner

harm   market   part

Reach Out for New Words

A   The words in the pictures need **ar**. Write each word. Then read the new words.

p__tner   h__m   c__pet

p__t   m__ket   t__get   c__d

1. c _____

2. c _____

3. t _____

4. p _____

5. m _____

6. p _____

7. h _____

B   Write the new **ar** words for the pictures.

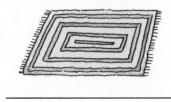  

1. _____   2. _____   3. _____

bee   seed   seem   tree
feel   week   street   feet
queen   sweet   free   meet

Practice the Words

A Write the spelling words. Circle the **ee** in each word.

1. bee

2.

3.

4.

5.

6.

7.

8.

9.

10.

11.

12.

B Find six **ee** words. Look across and down.
Circle the words. Write them on the lines.

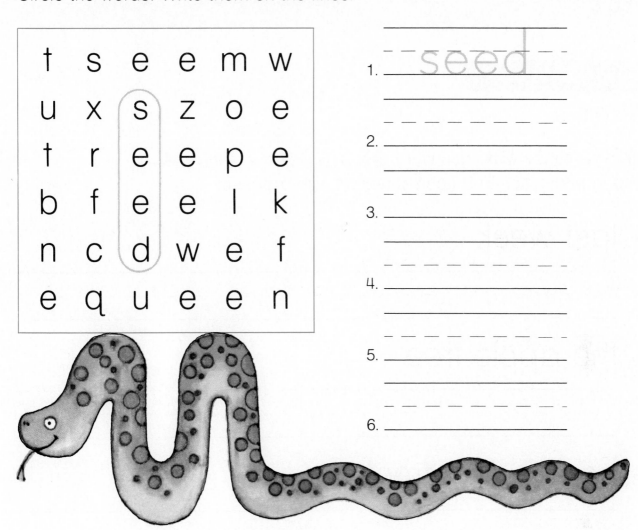

t	s	e	e	m	w
u	x	s	z	o	e
t	r	e	e	p	e
b	f	e	e	l	k
n	c	d	w	e	f
e	q	u	e	e	n

1. seed

2. _____

3. _____

4. _____

5. _____

6. _____

C Write the spelling words in sentences.

1. We will _m_____ this _w_____.

2. Is that a _q_____ _b_____?

3. Plant a _s_____ by the _t_____.

4. My _f_____ _f_____ cold.

bee   queen   week   street   feet   meet
feel   seed   seem   tree   free   sweet

Build Word Power

Writing

Write a sentence with each word group. Start each sentence with a capital letter. End each sentence with a period.

1. last week

2. the apple tree

3. across the street

4. to the queen

5. tastes sweet

 **My Dictionary**
Write your spelling words in **ABC** order.

 Words for Writing
Use **street** and **meet** in your writing.

screen   cheek   creep   greet

heel   speed   cheese

Reach Out for New Words

A Follow the directions to make new **ee** words.

1. Change the **f** in **feel** to **h**.

2. Change the **st** in **street** to **g**.

3. Change the **w** in **week** to **ch**.

4. Change the **qu** in **queen** to **scr**.

5. Change the **t** in **tree** to **c**.
   Add **p** at the end.

6. Put a **p** after the **s** in **seed**.

7. Change the **tr** in **tree** to **ch**.
   Add **se** at the end.

B Write the new **ee** words that go in the sentences.

1. A mouse likes to eat _____.

2. Her shoe needs a new _____.

3. Open the _____ door.

55

mean   peas   meat   eat
dream   bean   team   beat
leave   season   meal   seat

Practice the Words

A Write the spelling words. Circle the **ea** in each word.

1. mean   7.

2.   8.

3.   9.

4.   10.

5.   11.

6.   12.

B Write the **ea** word for each picture.

1. That is my _____ .

2. He had a funny _____ .

3. You will be late for the _____ .

4. She is on this _____ .

5. Bob likes to eat _____ .

Dictionary

C Write the three lists of words in alphabetical order.
In each list, the first three letters in each word are the
same. Alphabetize by using the fourth letter. Check your
order by looking for the words in the dictionary.

1

bean _____

beat _____

3

seat _____

season _____

2

meat _____

meal _____

mean	leave	bean	meat	eat	meal
dream	peas	season	team	beat	seat

Read the clues. Write the spelling words that fit in the puzzle.

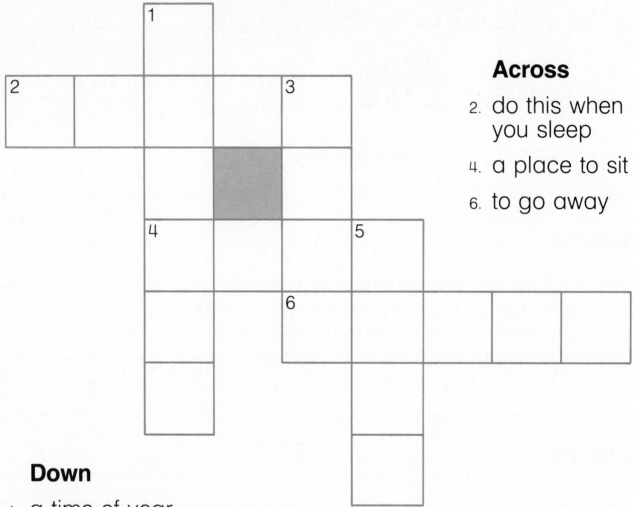

Across

2. do this when you sleep

4. a place to sit

6. to go away

Down

1. a time of year

3. breakfast, lunch, or dinner

5. all the players

My Dictionary
Write your spelling words in **ABC** order.

Words for Writing
Use **dream** and **mean** in your writing.

Reach Out for New Words

A Find the seven new **ea** words in the puzzle.
Circle each word. Write it on the line.

1. _____

2. _____

3. _____

4. _____

5. _____

6. _____

7. _____

B Write the new **ea** word that fits each clue.

1. not strong _____

2. large body of water _____

3. something warm _____

4. a water animal _____

5. not most _____

6. a small round thing _____

bell   well   smell   wall

add   egg   off   spill

less   doll   grass   will

Practice the Words

A Write the spelling words. Circle the double consonant endings.

1. _____   5. _____   9. _____

2. _____   6. _____   10. _____

3. _____   7. _____   11. _____

4. _____   8. _____   12. _____

B Write the spelling words that go in the sentences.

1. Four is _____ than five.

2. Can you _____ the flowers?

3. The baby might _____ the milk.

4. The book fell _____ the table.

5. _____ you help me?

6. I can _____ two plus five.

A <u>noun</u> is a word that names a person, a place, or a thing.
Father, **zoo**, and **apple** are nouns.

C Look at the words in the box. Write the words that are nouns.

bell   egg   doll   add   off   less   grass   wall

1. _____

2. _____

3. _____

4. _____

5. _____

Build Word Power

Make a sentence from each group of scrambled words.
The word with the capital letter will be the first word in each
sentence. Circle the spelling words.

1. flowers The smell nice.

2. you Can these add numbers?

3. has milk He less.

4. the spill water Don't.

5. want fry to I egg my.

My Dictionary
Write your spelling
words in **ABC** order.

Words for Writing
Use **bell** and **doll** in
your writing.

62

odd   buzz   hall   cuff   grill
dull   swell   purr   stuff

Reach Out for New Words

A Write the spelling words that have these letters.

ll   **dd**   **rr**

_____   _____   _____

- - - - - - -   - - - - - - -   - - - - - - -

_____   _____   _____

_____   _____

- - - - - - -   **ff**   **zz**

_____   _____   _____

_____   - - - - - - -   - - - - - - -

_____   _____   _____

- - - - - - -   _____

_____   - - - - - - -

                   _____

B Write the new words that go in the sentences. You will
need to add **s** or **ing** to some words.

1. The bump on my head is _____ .

2. Our school has two long _____ .

3. The bee is _____ around the flower.

4. We cooked hot dogs on the _____ .

5. The happy kitten is _____ .

63

just   best   fast   lost

most   must   west   east

last   list   past   against

Practice the Words

A Write the spelling words. Circle the **st** ending.

1. _____   7. _____

2. _____   8. _____

3. _____   9. _____

4. _____   10. _____

5. _____   11. _____

6. _____   12. _____

Some pairs of words tell about things that are different. These words are called <u>opposites</u>. **Hot** and **cold** are opposites.

B Write the spelling word that is the opposite of each word.

1. worst _____

2. fewest _____

3. first _____

4. found _____

5. east _____

6. slow _____

Dictionary

C Look at each pair of <u>guide words</u> below. What spelling words go with each pair of guide words? Write the words in alphabetical order. You may have to look at the second letter.

1. **after**	**funny**	2. **joke**	**lot**	3. **more**	**which**
_____		_____		_____	
_____		_____		_____	
_____		_____		_____	
_____		_____		_____	

Build Word Power

Writing

Write a sentence with each word group. Try to use other spelling words in your sentences.

1. just as fast

2. the best day

3. past the school

4. on the list

5. against the rules

 **My Dictionary**
Write your spelling words in **ABC** order.

 Words for Writing
Use **best** and **most** in your writing.

forest   cost   test   breakfast   feast   chest

Reach Out for New Words

A Find and write the new **st** words that fit in the puzzle.
The first word goes down.

1. _____

2. _____

3. _____

4. _____

5. _____

6. _____

B Write the new **st** words for the pictures.

1. _____ 2. _____ 3. _____

work + ing = working   work + ed = worked
need + ing = needing   need + ed = needed
miss + ing = missing   miss + ed = missed
help + ing = helping   help + ed = helped
want + ing = wanting   want + ed = wanted
jump + ing = jumping   jump + ed = jumped

A word that tells what someone or something does is a <u>verb</u>.
All the spelling words are verbs.
Add **ing** to show something is happening <u>now</u>.
Add **ed** to show something happened <u>before</u>.

Practice the Words

A Write the spelling words with the endings.

	Add **ing**	Add **ed**
1. work	working	worked
2. miss		
3. need		
4. help		
5. want		

A <u>base</u> <u>word</u> is the word you see before endings are added.

B Read the first word group after each number.
Make the second word group mean the
same thing. Add **ed** or **ing** to the <u>underlined</u>
base word. The first one is done to show you.

eat

1. asking for help   <u>need</u> needing help

2. working with friends   <u>help</u> _____ friends

3. was hungry   <u>want</u> _____ food

4. going over the rope   <u>jump</u> _____ rope

C Write the **ing** or **ed** word that goes in each sentence.

1. One part of the puzzle is _____.

2. They _____ a ticket to get in.

3. The class is _____ hard.

4. I _____ to go to the park today.

5. Al _____ Mom wash the dishes.

working	worked	helping	helped
needing	needed	jumping	jumped
missing	missed	wanting	wanted

Build Word Power

Proofreading

Cross out the spelling mistake in each sentence. Write each sentence correctly.

1. We needid you for the game.

2. She is helpin me read.

3. Kim wantd a hot dog.

4. My red mitten is mising.

My Dictionary
Write your spelling words in **ABC** order.

Words for Writing
Use **working** and **helped** in your writing.

Reach Out for New Words

A Add **ed** and **ing** to each word below. Watch for the
silent **e** words.

	Add **ed**	Add **ing**
1. call		
2. land		
3. mix		
4. rest		
5. paste		
6. bump		

B Write the new **ed** or **ing** words to match the pictures.

1. Ann ☎ Bill last night. _____

2. José 🛌 after the race. _____

3. The airplane is ✈ _____

paint dream wanted
leave large against
start last street
rain wall wait
less week jumping

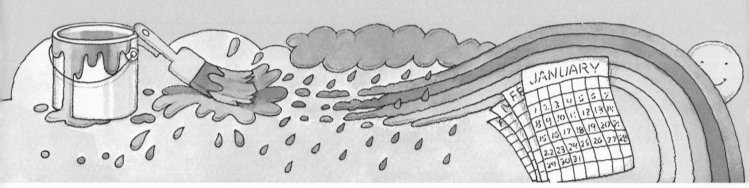

Practice

A Add the missing letters to make spelling words.

1. p __ __ nt
2. r __ __ n
3. l __ __ ge
4. w __ __ k
5. str __ __ t

6. l __ __ ve
7. le __ __
8. la __ __
9. w __ __ t
10. st __ __ t

11. dr __ __ m
12. wa __ __
13. again __ __
14. jump __ __ __
15. want __ __

72

B Write the spelling words for the pictures.

1. _____

2. _____

3. _____

4. _____

5. _____

6. _____

C Add **ed** and **ing** to these spelling words.

	ed	**ing**
1. paint	_____	_____
2. rain	_____	_____
3. last	_____	_____
4. want	_____	_____
5. wait	_____	_____
6. start	_____	_____
7. dream	_____	_____
8. jump	_____	_____

D Look at the words in the box. Some are <u>nouns</u> and some are <u>verbs</u>. Write the words under the correct heading.

Nouns	Verbs
1. _____	1. _____
2. _____	2. _____
3. _____	

More Practice

Dictionary

A Look at the <u>guide words</u> below. Write the words from the box that would go on the dictionary page with these guide words. Write the words in alphabetical order. You will not use all the words.

less   wall   wanting   large

wait   last   leave   week

1. **lamp**   **lemon**

_____

_____

_____

2. **walk**   **wet**

_____

_____

_____

Writing

B Write a sentence with each word group.

1. large building

_____

- -

_____

2. will leave

_____

- -

_____

3. less time

_____

- -

_____

4. against the curb

_____

- -

_____

C Circle the word in each line that is spelled correctly.

1. larje	large	larg
2. streat	strete	street
3. les	lese	less
4. wonted	wanted	wantid
5. wait	wate	wat
6. aginst	aganst	against

Sunday   November

Friday   December

Wednesday   January

Tuesday   February

Saturday   March

Monday

Thursday

Spell the Words

A Write the days of the week in order.

1. Sunday

2. _____

3. _____

4. _____

5. _____

6. _____

7. _____

B Write the days and months to fit the clues.

_____

1. before January

2. after Friday

3. before February

4. after Wednesday

5. before December

Proofreading

C Cross out the spelling mistake in each sentence. Write each sentence correctly.

1. There was snow in Febuary.

_____

2. Joe plays on Saterday.

_____

3. My birthday is in Januwary.

_____

Write With the Words

Help Becky and Jim plan their week with Aunt Sue. First choose a month. Write it in the first blank in the story. Then choose a day of the week. Write it in the second blank. Then on your own paper, write about what they did on that day and three other days.

Aunt Sue came to visit Becky and

Jim in _____. "Let's do

something special every day this week,"

she said.

"I thought _____ would be a

good day to _____."

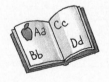

My Dictionary
Write your spelling words in **ABC** order.

Words for Writing
Use **Saturday** and **January** in your writing.

78

January	February	March	April
May	June	July	August
September	October	November	December

Learn More Words

Make a calendar for your birthday month.

1. Write the month on the top line.

2. Your teacher will tell you what day is the first day of that month. Write **1** under that day.

3. Find out how many days are in that month. Write a number for each day.

4. Draw a circle around your birthday.

SUNDAY	MONDAY	TUESDAY	WEDNESDAY	THURSDAY	FRIDAY	SATURDAY

what	*what*	when	*when*	which	*which*
whip	*whip*	why	*why*	where	*where*
white	*white*	while	*while*	whale	*whale*
wheel	*wheel*	whisper	*whisper*	whistle	*whistle*

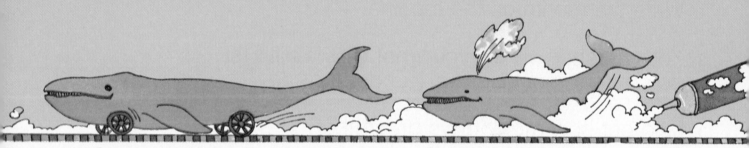

Practice the Words

A Write the five **wh** words that can begin a question.

1. _____ 3. _____ 5. _____

2. _____ 4. _____

Write the other **wh** words.

1. _____ 4. _____ 6. _____

2. _____ 5. _____ 7. _____

3. _____

B Write the **wh** words that fit in the shapes.

1.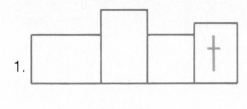

2.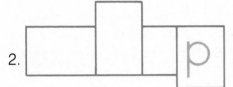

3.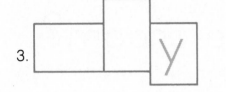

4.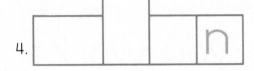

5.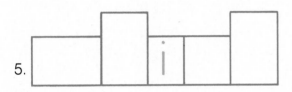

6.

7.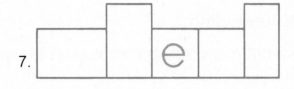

8.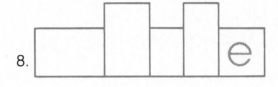

9.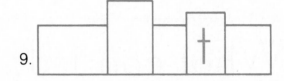

10.

C Write the **wh** words that go in the sentences.

1. Which _____ one did you eat?

2. Daisies are yellow and _____.

3. He blew the _____.

4. She will _____ in my ear.

Build Word Power

Proofreading

Cross out the spelling mistakes in the questions. Write the
words correctly.

1. Wen will you wip the cream?

   _____   _____
   - - - - - - -   - - - - - - -
   _____   _____

2. What can I do wile you work?

   _____
   - - - - - - -
   _____

3. Why did you wisper your name?

   _____
   - - - - - - -
   _____

4. Wher did the whale swim?

   _____
   - - - - - - -
   _____

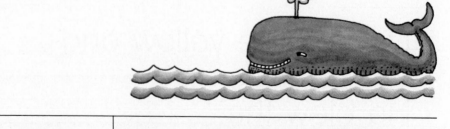

 **My Dictionary**
Write your spelling
words in **ABC** order.

 Words for Writing
Use **what** and **where** in
your writing.

82

wheat   whiskers   whiff   whine   whimper

Reach Out for New Words

A Read the directions. Write the new **wh** words.

1. Write the word that has a silent **e**.

2. Write the word that has the sound of long **e**.

3. Write the word that is plural.

4. Write the word that ends with **er**.

5. Write the word with a double consonant ending.

Writing

B Write a story about a dog on a farm. Use as many of the new **wh** words as you can. Remember to give your story a title.

she *she*   shake *shake*   shop *shop*

shove *shove*   fish *fish*   dash *dash*

push *push*   wash *wash*   rush *rush*

shoe *shoe*   sheet *sheet*   finish *finish*

Practice the Words

A Write the spelling words under the correct headings.

Beginning with **sh**

1. _____

2. _____

3. _____

4. _____

5. _____

6. _____

Ending with **sh**

7. _____

8. _____

9. _____

10. _____

11. _____

12. _____

Add **es** to verbs that end in **sh**.
This shows something that is happening <u>now</u>.

B Add **es** to the verbs ending in **sh**.

1. wash + es = _____

2. dash + es = _____

3. rush + es = _____

4. fish + es = _____

5. finish + es = _____

C Write the **sh** words that go in the sentences.

1. Susan said _____ will go.

2. Do I _____ or pull this door?

3. Put the clean _____ on the bed.

4. The man will _____ your hand.

5. Go into the _____ with me.

6. Where is my other brown _____?

Dictionary

A word you find in the dictionary is an <u>entry</u> <u>word</u>.
A <u>dictionary</u> <u>entry</u> tells you about the entry word.
The <u>definition</u>, or meaning of the word, may be given.
Some entries may also include a picture of the word.

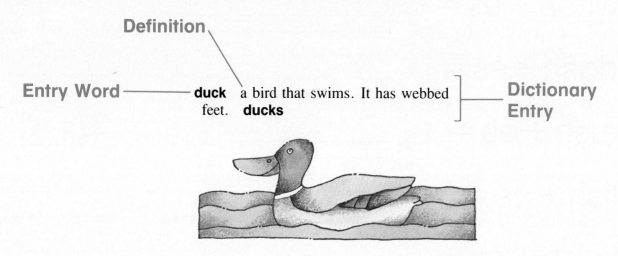

Definition

Entry Word ——————→ **duck** a bird that swims. It has webbed
feet. **ducks**

**Dictionary
Entry**

Find each entry word in your dictionary. Write the definition
of each word. Circle the word if it has a picture.

1. finish _____

2. shoe _____

3. dash _____

4. fish _____

My Dictionary
Write your spelling
words in **ABC** order.

Words for Writing
Use **push** and **shake** in
your writing.

Reach Out for New Words

A Circle the six **sh** words in the puzzle. Write the words.

1. _____

2. _____

3. _____

4. _____

5. _____

6. _____

B Add the missing letters to make the new **sh** words.

1. ___ o ___ ___ sh   4. sh a ___ ___

2. ___ ___ ___ ___ ___ sh   5. sh ___ ___ ___

3. ___ ___ ___ ___ sh   6. sh ___ ___ ___ ___

thank	*thank*	those	*those*	thing	*thing*
think	*think*	bath	*bath*	both	*both*
with	*with*	than	*than*	there	*there*
them	*them*	that	*that*	this	*this*

Practice the Words

A Write the spelling words. Circle the **th** in each word.

1. _____   5. _____   9. _____

2. _____   6. _____   10. _____

3. _____   7. _____   11. _____

4. _____   8. _____   12. _____

B Write the **th** words in the sentences.

1. _____ you for going to the store.

2. Our muddy dog needs a _____ .

3. We will go to the pool with _____ .

4. I like _____ of my friends.

5. Ann is taller _____ Kevin.

6. Put the book over _____ .

C Write the **th** word that rhymes with each word.

1. pink _____

2. ring _____

3. bank _____

4. stem _____

5. miss _____

6. cat _____

7. care _____

8. rose _____

Dictionary

Sometimes a dictionary entry will have a sentence that uses the entry word. This sentence helps you understand what the word means.

Definition

song music and words that you sing.

Sentence ——— We learned a *song* about spring.

songs

Find these words in your dictionary. Write the sentence that uses the word.

1. **think**

- -

2. **both**

- -

3. **thing**

- -

4. **thank**

- -

 **My Dictionary**
Write your spelling words in **ABC** order.

 Words for Writing
Use **this** and **thing** in your writing.

Reach Out for New Words

A Find the eight new **th** words in the puzzle.
Look across and down. Circle the words.
Write them on the lines.

```
a  t  o  g  e  t  h  e  r
r  o  g  a  t  h  e  r  p
i  t  e  b  o  o  t  h  a
t  h  r  c  o  r  t  h  t
h  e  a  r  b  x  l  t  h
m  r  n  o  t  h  i  n  g
e  o  b  m  o  r  o  p  q
t  r  o  a  t  t  r  w  h
i  s  o  t  t  m  w  z  e
c  v  x  h  w  h  o  p  l
```

1. _____

2. _____

3. _____

4. _____

5. _____

6. _____

7. _____

8. _____

B Write the new **th** words in alphabetical order.

1. _____

2. _____

3. _____

4. _____

5. _____

6. _____

7. _____

8. _____

chat *chat*   chop *chop*   child *child*

chin *chin*   such *such*   much *much*

each *each*   bunch *bunch*   pinch *pinch*

chair *chair*   reach *reach*   chew *chew*

Practice the Words

A Write the spelling words under the correct headings.

Beginning with **ch**

_____

1. _____

2. _____

3. _____

4. _____

5. _____

6. _____

Ending with **ch**

_____

7. _____

8. _____

9. _____

10. _____

11. _____

12. _____

B Write the **ch** words for the pictures.

1. _____

2. _____

3. _____

4. _____

C Write the **ch** words that rhyme with each word.

1. fat _____

2. much _____

3. fair _____

4. lunch _____

5. each _____

6. wild _____

7. top _____

8. inch _____

9. such _____

10. flew _____

Build Word Power

Make the word groups into sentences. Start each sentence
with a capital letter. End each sentence with a period.
Circle the **ch** words.

1. shoes these pinch feet my

2. fun such was it

3. broken chair is the

4. his he chin hit

5. it you can reach

My Dictionary
Write your spelling
words in **ABC** order.

Words for Writing
Use **chat** and **child** in
your writing.

94

crunch   lunch   chip   beach

chance   spinach   cheer   church

Reach Out for New Words

A Answer the riddles with new **ch** words.

1. I'm the meal you eat at noon. _____

2. I'm the brown bit in some cookies. _____

3. I'm a place to swim. _____

4. I'm a building where people pray. _____

5. I am a happy feeling. _____

6. I'm a green vegetable. _____

7. I may or may not happen. _____

8. I'm a sound you make when you bite. _____

B Write the new **ch** words for the pictures.

1. _____   2. _____   3. _____

back	*back*	pick	*pick*	duck	*duck*
neck	*neck*	kick	*kick*	rocket	*rocket*
thick	*thick*	trick	*trick*	sock	*sock*
black	*black*	block	*block*	ticket	*ticket*

Practice the Words

A Write the **ck** words in alphabetical order. You will have to look at the second or third letter in some words.

1. _____ 5. _____ 9. _____

2. _____ 6. _____ 10. _____

3. _____ 7. _____ 11. _____

4. _____ 8. _____ 12. _____

B The words below have endings added. Write the spelling words without the endings.

1. picked _____

2. kicking _____

3. tricked _____

4. ducks _____

5. socks _____

6. necks _____

7. blocked _____

8. backs _____

9. rockets _____

Dictionary

C Look up each word below in your dictionary. Then write the entry word under the correct heading.

| duck | neck | rocket | sock | thick | ticket |

Sentence Clue

_____

_____

_____

_____

Picture Clue

_____

_____

back   ticket   pick   trick   rocket   block

neck   black   kick   duck   sock   thick

Build Word Power

Proofreading

Read each sentence. Cross out the misspelled word. Write the sentence correctly.

1. Go bak to the line.

_____

2. Did you hurt your nec?

_____

3. Pik the book you want.

_____

4. The blak cat is soft.

_____

5. The roket went into the sky.

_____

 **My Dictionary**
Write your spelling words in **ABC** order.

 Words for Writing
Use **back** and **neck** in your writing.

Reach Out for New Words

A Follow the directions to make the new **ck** words.

1. Change the **th** in **thick** to **st**.

2. Change the **bl** in **black** to **qu**.

3. Change the **r** in **rocket** to **p**.

4. Change the **p** in **pick** to **n** and add **el** at the end.

5. Change the **bl** in **black** to **cr**.

6. Change the **n** in **neck** to **ch**.

B Write the new **ck** words for the pictures. Add the endings.

1. 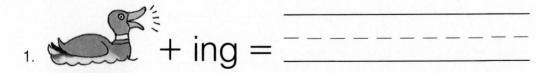 + ing = _____

2. + s = _____

3. + ed = _____

deep deeper deepest   new   newer   newest
tall taller tallest   green greener greenest
slow slower slowest   short shorter shortest

Add **er** to base words to mean <u>more</u>.

deep
deeper

Add **est** to base words to mean <u>most</u>. **deepest**

Practice the Words

A Write the spelling words that mean <u>more</u>.

1. _____   4. _____

2. _____   5. _____

3. _____   6. _____

B Write the spelling words that mean <u>most</u>.

_____   _____

1. _____   4. _____

_____   _____

2. _____   5. _____

_____   _____

3. _____   6. _____

C Read the sentences. Write the **er** or **est** word that the picture shows.

Andy   **Dave**   **Kim**

1. Andy is _____ than Kim.

2. Dave is the _____ boy.

3. Kim has the _____ shirt.

Build Word Power

Write the word that fits in the shapes.
Add **er** or **est** to each word below.

1. short

2. slow

3. tall

4. green

5. new

6. deep

My Dictionary
Write your spelling
words in **ABC** order.

Words for Writing
Use **tallest** and **slowest** in
your writing.

Reach Out for New Words

A Complete the chart with the base, **er**, and **est** forms of each word.

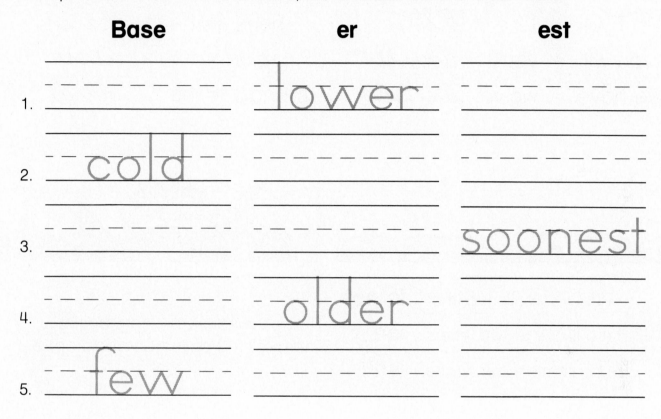

	Base	er	est
1.		lower	
2.	cold		
3.			soonest
4.		older	
5.	few		

Writing

B Write a sentence with each word.

1. old

2. lowest

is not = isn't   *isn't*   she will = she'll   *she'll*

can not = can't   *can't*   I am = I'm   *I'm*

are not = aren't   *aren't*   you are = you're   *you're*

I will = I'll   *I'll*   he is = he's   *he's*

you will = you'll   *you'll*   it is = it's   *it's*

we have = we've   *we've*   he had = he'd   *he'd*

Put two words together. **is not**

Take out one or two letters. **isn o t**

Put a mark in the space. **isn't**

The word is called a <u>contraction</u>.
The mark ' is called an <u>apostrophe</u>.

Practice the Words

A Write the contractions.

1. _____   5. _____   9. _____

2. _____   6. _____   10. _____

3. _____   7. _____   11. _____

4. _____   8. _____   12. _____

B Draw a line to match the words and contractions. Cross out the letter or letters left out when you write the contraction.

1. I will	I'll	
2. is not	I'm	
3. I am	we've	
4. she will	can't	
5. can not	isn't	
6. we have	she'll	

1. you are	he's	
2. are not	you're	
3. he is	aren't	
4. you will	he'd	
5. it is	you'll	
6. he had	it's	

C Write the contractions. Show the letters that are missing.

'll ending	Missing Letters	't ending	Missing Letters
I'll	wi		

| isn't | aren't | I'll | she'll | he's | we've |
| can't | you'll | I'm | you're | it's | he'd |

Build Word Power

Circle the words that you can make into contractions.
Write the contractions.

1. (She will) go home. _she'll_

2. It is a new game.

3. I will run now.

4. I am staying here.

5. You are very nice.

6. He can not jump.

7. We have seen the play.

8. He is playing.

 **My Dictionary**
Write your spelling
words in **ABC** order.

 Words for Writing
Use **I'll** and **I'm** in
your writing.

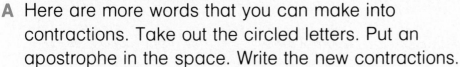

we'll   that's   didn't   I've   he'll

Reach Out for New Words

A Here are more words that you can make into
contractions. Take out the circled letters. Put an
apostrophe in the space. Write the new contractions.

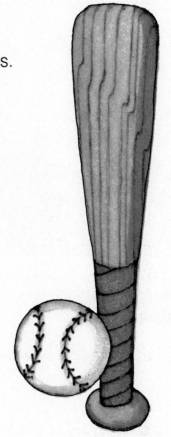

1. did n⊙t _____

2. that ⓘs _____

3. I ⟨have⟩ _____

4. he ⟨will⟩ _____

5. we ⟨will⟩ _____

B Change the underlined words to contractions. Write each
sentence.

1. They <u>did not</u> go to the game.

_____

2. <u>We will</u> go on Monday.

_____

rocket *rocket*   shorter *shorter*   with *with*
there *there*   greenest *greenest*   shoe *shoe*
aren't *aren't*   finish *finish*   when *when*
each *each*   trick *trick*   chair *chair*
where *where*   we've *we've*   you're *you're*

Practice

A Write the spelling words that have these letters.

sh

_____

_____

_____

_____

wh

_____

_____

_____

th

_____

_____

_____

ch

_____

_____

_____

ck

_____

_____

_____

B Change the base form of the words to new forms. Follow the directions.

_____

1. shoe   Write the plural form.   _____

2. finish   Write the **es** form.   _____

3. short   Write the **er** form.   _____

4. trick   Write the **ing** form.   _____

5. green   Write the **est** form.   _____

Dictionary

C Look at the three word lists. Number the words in each list in alphabetical order.

1	**2**	**3**
where ___	when ___	with ___
there ___	each ___	aren't ___
rocket _1_	shorter ___	chair ___
shoe ___	greenest ___	trick ___
you're ___	we've ___	finish ___

D Write the contraction for the words.

1. are not _____

3. we have _____

2. you are _____

A Look up these words in your dictionary. Write the sentence clue for each entry.

1. where

_____
_____

2. chair

_____
_____

3. each

_____
_____

4. trick

_____
_____

5. there

_____
_____

Proofreading

B Read each sentence. Cross out the spelling mistakes.
Then write each sentence correctly.

1. Wen did you find your shoe?

_____

2. Eech of us will finish the race.

_____

3. Youre shorter than Jim.

_____

4. Wher did the roket go?

_____

C Four of the words in the box will fit in the shapes. Find
and write those words.

| trick | when | shorter | each |
| chair | shoe | greenest | there |

1.

2.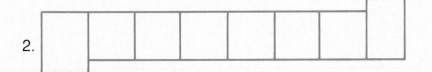

3.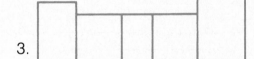

4.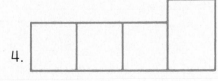

my	*my*	your	*your*	his	*his*
mine	*mine*	yours	*yours*	their	*their*
our	*our*	her	*her*	theirs	*theirs*
ours	*ours*	hers	*hers*	its	*its*

These spelling words can be used to show that a thing belongs to someone or something.

This <u>book belongs to me.</u>

This is <u>my</u> book.

This book is <u>mine.</u>

These words are called <u>possessive pronouns.</u>

Spell the Words

A Write the possessive pronouns.

1. _____   5. _____   9. _____

2. _____   6. _____   10. _____

3. _____   7. _____   11. _____

4. _____   8. _____   12. _____

B Write one or two spelling words to fit each clue.

1. belongs to **him**

_____

_____

5. belongs to **them**

_____   _____

_____   _____

2. belongs to **it**

_____

_____

6. belongs to **you**

_____   _____

_____   _____

3. belongs to **her**

_____   _____

_____   _____

7. belongs to **us**

_____   _____

_____   _____

4. belongs to **me**

_____   _____

_____   _____

Writing

C Rewrite each sentence in two ways. Use two different spelling words in place of the underlined words.

1. That house <u>belongs to us</u>.

That house is ours.

That is our house.

2. This pencil <u>belongs to me</u>.

_____

_____

_____

_____

113

Write With the Words

Write the correct pronouns in the story. Then write an ending for the story on your paper. Where did Juan and Nancy have the party? What games did they play?

Juan and Nancy were planning a party for _____ friend Anna. They wanted to surprise Anna on _____ birthday.

"Should we have the party at _____ house or _____ house?" Juan asked Nancy.

Nancy said, "_____."

My Dictionary
Write your spelling words in **ABC** order.

Words for Writing
Use **my** and **our** in your writing.

yourself   myself   itself   herself   ourselves

Learn More Words

A Write the new pronoun that goes with the underlined word.

When you write a sentence, you can: _____

1. use this word with <u>I</u>.   _____

2. use this word with <u>you</u>.   _____

3. use this word with <u>her</u>.   _____

4. use this word with <u>us</u>.   _____

5. use this word with <u>it</u>.   _____

B Write the new words that go in the sentences.

1. I can do it by _____ .

2. The kitten got _____ out of the tree.

3. She wrote the letter _____ .

4. We helped _____ to dinner.

5. Did you paint the roof _____ ?

bird *bird*   stir *stir*   circle *circle*

girl *girl*   shirt *shirt*   skirt *skirt*

sir *sir*   firm *firm*   thirsty *thirsty*

dirt *dirt*   chirp *chirp*   birthday *birthday*

Practice the Words

A Write the spelling words. Circle the **ir** in each word.

1. bird

2. _____

3. _____

4. _____

5. _____

6. _____

7. _____

8. _____

9. _____

10. _____

11. _____

12. _____

B Write the **ir** words for the pictures.

1. _____

2. _____

3. _____

4. _____

5. _____

Proofreading

C Cross out the misspelled words in each sentence. Then write the words correctly.

1. Stur water and dert together.

_____ _____

_____ _____

2. The thersty bird will churp.

_____ _____

_____ _____

3. I got a shurt for my berthday.

_____ _____

_____ _____

Build Word Power

Sometimes one word will make you think of another word.
Look at the words below. Each word should make you think
of a spelling word. Write the spelling word that fits each clue.

1. round _circle_

2. tweet _____

3. robin _____

4. mix _____

5. soil _____

6. hard _____

7. man _____

8. dress _____

9. drink _____

10. age _____

11. blouse _____

12. woman _____

My Dictionary
Write your spelling
words in **ABC** order.

Words for Writing
Use **shirt** and **skirt** in
your writing.

118

dirty   twirl   circus   squirted   squirm   fir

Reach Out for New Words

A Follow the directions to make the new **ir** words.

1. Change the **sk** in **skirt** to **d**.
   Add **y** at the end.

2. Change the **s** in **sir** to **f**.

3. Change the **f** in **firm** to **squ**.

4. Change the **s** in **sir** to **c**.
   Add **cus** at the end.

5. Change the **g** in **girl** to **tw**.

6. Change the **k** in **skirt** to **qu**.
   Add **ed** at the end.

B Write the new **ir** words that fit in the shapes.

1.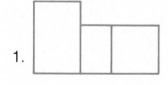

2.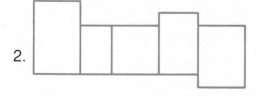

3.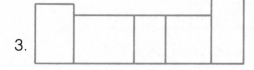

4.

5.

blow *blow*   shadow *shadow*   owner *owner*

row *row*   throw *throw*   crows *crows*

bow *bow*   window *window*   grow *grow*

show *show*   elbow *elbow*   snow *snow*

Practice the Words

A Write the **ow** words in alphabetical order. Circle the **ow** in each word.

1. _____

2. _____

3. _____

4. _____

5. _____

6. _____

7. _____

8. _____

9. _____

10. _____

11. _____

12. _____

B Write the **ow** words that fit the clues.

1. the wind can do this _____

2. something to tie _____

3. a place to look out _____

4. a rooster does this _____

5. toss to someone _____

6. to get taller _____

7. body part _____

C Write the ten spelling words that end in **ow**.

1. _____   5. _____   9. _____

2. _____   6. _____   10. _____

3. _____   7. _____

4. _____   8. _____

Dictionary

An entry word in the dictionary is usually the <u>base form</u> of that word. Other <u>forms</u> of that word may be shown in the entry. These forms may have endings.

entry word ——— **bake** to cook in an oven. *Bake* the cookies for ten minutes. **baked, baking** ——— **forms of the entry word**

Find each word below in your dictionary. Write all the word forms you find in the entry.

1. row

2. elbow

3. show

4. window

5. snow

Two of your spelling words are <u>not</u> base forms. Write the base form of each word. Use your dictionary to help you.

1. owner

2. crows

My Dictionary
Write your spelling words in **ABC** order.

Words for Writing
Use **shadow** and **window** in your writing.

tomorrow   Halloween   bowl   borrow   pillow   narrow

Reach Out for New Words

A Write the new **ow** words that fit the clues.

1. a night for costumes _____

2. after today _____

3. a dish for cereal _____

4. put it under your head _____

5. take for a short time _____

6. very thin _____

Writing

B Write a sentence with each word group.

1. a soft pillow
_____
_____

2. on Halloween
_____
_____

3. tomorrow morning
_____
_____

brown	*brown*	now	*now*	owl	*owl*
cow	*cow*	crowd	*crowd*	town	*town*
shower	*shower*	down	*down*	how	*how*
towel	*towel*	crown	*crown*	frown	*frown*

Practice the Words

a b c d e f g h i j k l m n o p q r s t u v w x y z

A Write the **ow** words in alphabetical order. Some words begin with the same letters. Look at the other letters.

1. _____

2. _____

3. _____

4. _____

5. _____

6. _____

7. _____

8. _____

9. _____

10. _____

11. _____

12. _____

124

B Write the **ow** words for the pictures.

1. _____

2. _____

3. _____

4. _____

5. _____

6. _____

Dictionary

C Find these words in your dictionary. Write all the word forms
you find in the entry for each word.

1. crowd _____ _____

2. crown _____ _____

3. frown _____ _____

4. brown _____ _____

Build Word Power

Writing

Write a sentence with each pair of words.

1. brown, cow

----

2. shower, towel

----

3. crown, now

----

4. town, crowd

----

5. frown, how

 **My Dictionary**
Write your spelling
words in **ABC** order.

 Words for Writing
Use **cow** and **town** in
your writing.

bow   powder   however   howl   plow   gown   vowel

Reach Out for New Words

A Circle the **ow** in each word. Then write the word.

1. powder _____   5. howl _____

2. gown _____   6. bow _____

3. vowel _____   7. plow _____

4. however _____

Writing

B Write a sentence with each word group.

1. a long gown

_____

2. took a bow

_____

3. likes to howl

_____

4. a vowel in

_____

apart *apart*   alive *alive*   alone *alone*

awake *awake*   asleep *asleep*   ago *ago*

awhile *awhile*   again *again*   along *along*

above *above*   away *away*   alike *alike*

Practice the Words

A Write the spelling words. Circle the beginning letter **a** in each word.

1. _____   5. _____   9. _____

2. _____   6. _____   10. _____

3. _____   7. _____   11. _____

4. _____   8. _____   12. _____

B Look at the picture. Write the spelling words that go in the sentences.

1. The bird is _____ the tree.

2. A tree is _____ the side of the road.

3. The rabbit is far _____ from the bird.

Dictionary

C Write the spelling words that go under the correct guide words. Put them in alphabetical order.

alike	among	about	ahead

apart   awhile   alive   again   alone   along

awake   above   asleep   away   ago   alike

Build Word Power

Write the spelling words to finish the story.

     A long time __1__ there was a little dog that had no owner. He lived all __2__. He decided to run __3__ from the city. He walked __4__ busy streets. He got tired and fell __5__ for __6__. Soon he opened his eyes. He saw two girls who looked __7__. They were twins. They said, "Now you will have two owners!"

1. _____   4. _____   7. _____

2. _____   5. _____

3. _____   6. _____

My Dictionary

Write your spelling words in **ABC** order.

Words for Writing

Use **awake** and **asleep** in your writing.

Reach Out for New Words

A Can you find the six new **a** words in this puzzle? Circle and write the words. Look for the beginning letter **a**.

v a h e a d a r o u n d u v l a

1. _____

2. _____

3. _____

4. _____

5. _____

6. _____

B Write the new **a** words that fit the clues.

1. To use a bridge is to go _____ it.

2. Two people both like something. They _____.

3. To be the leader in a race is to be _____.

4. To tell something is to talk _____ it.

before	*before*	beside	*beside*
became	*became*	between	*between*
belong	*belong*	become	*become*
begin	*begin*	below	*below*
began	*began*	because	*because*
behind	*behind*	beyond	*beyond*

Practice the Words

A Write the spelling words. Circle the **be** at the beginning of each word.

1. _____

2. _____

3. _____

4. _____

5. _____

6. _____

7. _____

8. _____

9. _____

10. _____

11. _____

12. _____

B Add the missing vowels to make each word.
Circle the words that have a silent **e** at the end.

1. b __ f __ r __

2. b __ y __ nd

3. b __ cam __

4. b __ s __ d __

5. b __ c __ __ s __

6. b __ gan

7. b __ h __ nd

8. b __ tw __ __ n

Dictionary

C Write these spelling words in alphabetical order.

belong	beside	beyond	begin	become

1. _____

2. _____

3. _____

4. _____

5. _____

before   belong began beside   become   because
became begin   behind between below   beyond

Build Word Power

Look at the picture. Write the words that go in the sentences.

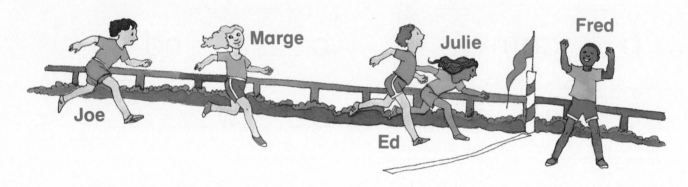

1. Julie will reach the end _____ Ed.

2. Marge is _____ Ed and Joe.

3. Joe is _____ all the others.

4. Ed is _____ Julie.

5. The road is _____ their feet.

6. Fred is _____ the finish line.

 **My Dictionary**
Write your spelling
words in **ABC** order.

 Words for Writing
Use **before** and **became** in
your writing.

beware   beneath   believe   begun   behave

Reach Out for New Words

A Find the missing consonants. Write each word.

1. __ e __ h a __ e   4. __ e __ u __

2. __ e __ ie __ e   5. __ e __ a __ e

3. __ e __ ea __ __

B Write the new **be** words that go in the sentences.

1. The sign said, " B_____ of the dog."

2. Look _____ the rug.

3. I _____ you can do it.

4. Have you _____ to study?

5. We will _____ in school today.

135

better	*better*	rabbit	*rabbit*
hammer	*hammer*	button	*button*
bottom	*bottom*	hello	*hello*
mitten	*mitten*	yellow	*yellow*
scatter	*scatter*	sudden	*sudden*
kitten	*kitten*	letter	*letter*

Practice the Words

A Write the words. Circle the double consonant in each word.

1. _____   7. _____

2. _____   8. _____

3. _____   9. _____

4. _____   10. _____

5. _____   11. _____

6. _____   12. _____

B Write the spelling words that have these letters.

tt

_____

_____

_____

_____

_____

_____

_____

_____

_____

_____

ll

_____

_____

_____

_____

mm

_____

_____

bb

_____

_____

dd

_____

_____

Proofreading

C Cross out the spelling mistake in each sentence. Write the sentence correctly.

1. My kiten is gray and white.

_____

_____

2. The rabitt hopped by the tree.

_____

_____

better	bottom	scatter	rabbit	hello	sudden
hammer	mitten	kitten	button	yellow	letter

Build Word Power

Read the clues. Write the spelling words that go in the puzzle.

Across

2. opposite of **top**

4. keeps your coat closed

5. say this to someone

Down

1. a baby cat

2. nicer

3. wear on your hand

My Dictionary

Write your spelling words in **ABC** order.

Words for Writing

Use **kitten** and **rabbit** in your writing.

138

Reach Out for New Words

A Follow the directions. Then write the new words.

1. Color the words with **tt** in red.

   _____   _____   _____

   _____   _____   _____

2. Color the word with **ss** in yellow.

   _____

   _____

3. Color the words with **bb** and **nn** in green.

   _____   _____

   _____   _____

   _____   _____

pattern

blossom

matter   lettuce

rubber   manner

Writing

B Write a sentence to answer each question. Use one of the new words in each of your answers.

1. Is anything wrong?

   _____

   _____

2. What is on your sandwich?

   _____

   _____

3. What is that toy made of?

   _____

   _____

139

base + ball	=	baseball	*baseball*
some + thing	=	something	*something*
down + hill	=	downhill	*downhill*
snow + ball	=	snowball	*snowball*
in + to	=	into	*into*
bed + time	=	bedtime	*bedtime*
pan + cake	=	pancake	*pancake*
book + case	=	bookcase	*bookcase*
home + sick	=	homesick	*homesick*
rain + bow	=	rainbow	*rainbow*
with + out	=	without	*without*
foot + ball	=	football	*football*

Some words are made by putting two words together.
These words are called <u>compound words</u>.

Practice the Words

A Write the spelling words in alphabetical order.

1. _____   7. _____

2. _____   8. _____

3. _____   9. _____

4. _____   10. _____

5. _____   11. _____

6. _____   12. _____

B Write the spelling words for the pictures.

1. _____

2. _____

3. _____

4. _____

5. _____

6. _____

C Make compound words. Add one word to each word below.

1. snow _____

2. bed _____

3. rain _____

4. in _____

5. home _____

6. with _____

7. book _____

8. some _____

9. pan _____

10. down _____

baseball	downhill	bedtime	bookcase
something	snowball	pancake	football
without	rainbow	homesick	into

Build Word Power

Write the word for each picture. Then write the compound
word made from the two words.

1. _____ + _____ = _____

2. _____ + _____ = _____

3. _____ + _____ = _____

4. _____ + _____ = _____

 **My Dictionary**
Write your spelling
words in **ABC** order.

 Words for Writing
Use **something** and
rainbow in your writing.

doghouse snowman storybook raindrop
doorbell anything anybody airplane

Reach Out for New Words

A Look at these silly compound words. Write the real compound that begins with the underlined word.

1. <u>dog</u>bell _____

5. <u>door</u>book _____

2. <u>snow</u>thing _____

6. <u>any</u>man _____

3. <u>story</u>drop _____

7. <u>any</u>plane _____

4. <u>rain</u>house _____

8. <u>air</u>body _____

B Write the new compound words that fit the clues.

1. place for a pet _____

2. something to read _____

3. one person _____

4. you ring it _____

5. make one in winter _____

6. people fly in it _____

button	*button*	towel	*towel*	again	*again*
window	*window*	awhile	*awhile*	chirp	*chirp*
hammer	*hammer*	before	*before*	better	*better*
bookcase	*bookcase*	rainbow	*rainbow*	throw	*throw*
because	*because*	shower	*shower*	circle	*circle*

Practice

A Add the missing vowels to make spelling words.

1. b __ t t __ n

2. b __ f __ r __

3. ch __ r p

4. t h r __ w

5. t __ w __ l

6. c __ r c l __

7. __ g __ n

8. b __ c __ __ s __

9. __ w h __ l __

10. h __ m m __ r

11. r __ __ n b __ w

12. b __ __ k c __ s __

13. b __ t t __ r

14. w __ n d __ w

15. s h __ w __ r

144

Dictionary

B Number the words in each list in alphabetical order.

1

awhile ___

before ___

better ___

again ___

because ___

bookcase ___

2

towel ___

rainbow ___

chirp ___

throw ___

circle ___

shower ___

C Write the words that go in the sentences.

1. A _____ fell off my coat.

2. Use a _____ to hit the nail.

3. Draw a big, round _____.

4. Get a _____ to dry the wet dish.

5. We saw a pretty _____ in the sky.

D Cross out the misspelled word in each group. Then write the word correctly.

1. towel
   cercle
   before

   _____

   _ _ _ _ _ _ _ _ _

   _____

2. better
   hamer
   button

   _____

   _ _ _ _ _ _ _ _ _

   _____

3. again
   throw
   befor

   _____

   _ _ _ _ _ _ _ _ _

   _____

More Practice

Dictionary

A Find each base word in your dictionary. Write the other word forms you see in the entry.

1. towel

   _____

   _ _ _ _ _ _ _ _ _

   _____

3. button

   _____

   _ _ _ _ _ _ _ _ _

   _____

5. shower

   _____

   _ _ _ _ _ _ _ _ _

   _____

2. throw

   _____

   _ _ _ _ _ _ _ _ _

   _____

   _____

4. chirp

   _____

   _ _ _ _ _ _ _ _ _

   _____

   _____

chirp   throw   button   shower

B Write the words that go in the sentences. You will need to add endings to each word. Use the endings **s**, **ed**, and **ing**.

1. Katie is _____ the ball.

2. We have two _____ in our house.

3. The bird has _____ all day.

4. His shirt has five _____ .

C Write the spelling words that fit the clues.

1. a shape

2. used for drying

3. once more

4. in front of

5. a place for books

6. colors in the sky

7. has glass in it

eighteen	*eighteen*	thirteen	*thirteen*
fourteen	*fourteen*	nineteen	*nineteen*
fifteen	*fifteen*	seventeen	*seventeen*
fifty	*fifty*	seventy	*seventy*
thirty	*thirty*	twenty	*twenty*
sixty	*sixty*	eighty	*eighty*

Spell the Words

A Write the spelling word for each numeral.

30 _____   14 _____

13 _____   70 _____

80 _____   17 _____

15 _____   60 _____

20 _____   19 _____

18 _____   50 _____

B Write the spelling words under the correct heading.

<table>
<tr><td colspan="2" align="center">End with **teen**</td><td colspan="2" align="center">End with **ty**</td></tr>
<tr><td>1.</td><td>_____</td><td>1.</td><td>_____</td></tr>
<tr><td>2.</td><td>_____</td><td>2.</td><td>_____</td></tr>
<tr><td>3.</td><td>_____</td><td>3.</td><td>_____</td></tr>
<tr><td>4.</td><td>_____</td><td>4.</td><td>_____</td></tr>
<tr><td>5.</td><td>_____</td><td>5.</td><td>_____</td></tr>
<tr><td>6.</td><td>_____</td><td>6.</td><td>_____</td></tr>
</table>

C Write the number words that answer the questions.

1. What is ten + ten? _____

2. What is twenty − two? _____

3. What is forty − ten? _____

4. What is sixty + twenty? _____

5. What is twelve + one? _____

6. What is twenty − one? _____

eighteen   fifty   thirteen   seventy   fifteen   sixty
fourteen   thirty   nineteen   twenty   seventeen   eighty

Write With the Words

Write the spelling word that matches each numeral in the story. Then write your own ending for the story. What do you think happened next?

Last summer, we drove (80) _____

_____ miles to my Uncle John's

house near the lake. We had a birthday

party for my cousin Pat. She is (13)

_____

_____ years old. Her brother,

Scott, is (15) _____. We went

_____

sailing in their new boat. _____

My Dictionary
Write your spelling words in **ABC** order.

Words for Writing
Use **fifteen** and **fifty** in your writing.

150

thirty-three   forty-four   ninety-two

eighty-one   twenty-two   fifty-five

Learn More Words

A Write the new number words for each numeral.

1. 44 _____

2. 92 _____

3. 81 _____

4. 33 _____

5. 22 _____

6. 55 _____

B Write one of the new number words for each silly sentence. You decide which number should go in each sentence.

1. My new chair has _____ legs.

2. The baby weighs _____ pounds.

3. I ate _____ hamburgers for lunch.

4. Our house has _____ windows.

5. I am _____ years old.

6. You must be _____ years old.

Aa

above _____

add _____

again _____

against _____

ago _____

aim _____

alike _____

alive _____

alone _____

along _____

any _____

apart _____

aren't _____

art _____

as _____

asleep _____

awake _____

away

awhile

Bb

back

bake

baking

bang

barn

baseball

bath

bean

beat

became

because

become

bedtime

bee

before

began

begin

behind

bell

belong

below

beside

best

better

between

beyond

bike

biking

bird

birthday

black

block

blow

blue

book

bookcase

boot

both

bottom

bow

bring

broke

brook

brown

bunch

button

by

Cc

came

can't

car

chair

chat

chew

child

chin

chirp

chop

circle

cook

cow

crowd

crown

crows

cry

Dd

dash

date

December

deep

deeper

deepest

dirt

dive

diving

doll

down

downhill

dream

duck

Ee

each

east

eat

egg

eight

eighteen

eighty

elbow

eleven

Ff

far

farm

fast

February

feel

feet

fifteen _____

fifty _____

finish _____

firm _____

fish _____

five _____

food _____

fool _____

foot _____

football _____

four _____

fourteen _____

free _____

Friday _____

frown _____

Gg

gave _____

girl _____

good _____

grade _____

grass _____

gray _____

green _____

greener _____

greenest

grow

Hh

hammer

hang

hard

has

he'd

he's

hello

help

helped

helping

her

hers

hide

hiding

him

his

homesick

hood

hook

hope

hoping

how

I i

I'll

I'm

if

into

isn't

it

it's

its

J j

January

job

joke

joking

jump

jumped

jumping

just

K k

kick

king

kitten

L l

large

last

leave

less

letter

list

long

look

loose

lost

Mm

made

mail

make

making

many

March

mark

may

meal

mean

meat

meet

mine

miss

missed

missing

mitten

Monday

moon

most

much

must

my

Nn

nail

name

naming

neck

need

needed

needing

new

newer

newest

nine

nineteen

noon

not

note

November

now

Oo

off

one

only

our

ours

owl

owner

Pp

paid

paint

pancake

park

past

peas

pick

pie

pinch

plain

pool

praise

push

Qq

queen

Rr

rabbit

race

racing

rain

rainbow

reach

red

ring

rocket

room

rope

roping

row

rule

ruling

run

rush

Ss

sail

Saturday

scatter

school

season

seat

seed

seem

seven

seventeen

seventy

shadow

shake

sharp

she

she'll

sheet

shirt

shoe

shop

short

shorter

shortest

shove

show

shower

shy

side

sing

sir

six

sixty

skirt

sky

slow

slower

slowest

smell

snow

snowball

sock

something

song

spill

spring

start

stir

stood

street

strong

such

sudden

Sunday

sweet

swing

T t

tail

tall

taller

tallest

team

ten

than

thank

that

their

theirs

them

there

these

thick

thing

think

thirsty

thirteen

thirty

this

those

three

throw

Thursday

ticket

today

too

took

tooth

towel

town

trail

tree

trick

Tuesday

twelve

twenty

twice

two

Uu

up

us

use

using

Vv

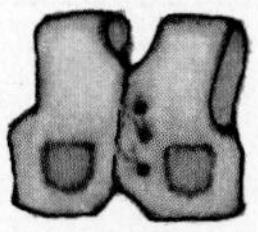

very

Ww

wait

wall

want

wanted

wanting

wash

way

we've

Wednesday

week

well

west

whale

what

wheel

when

where

which

while

whip

whisper

whistle

white

why

will

window

wing

with

without

wood

wool

work

worked

working

X x

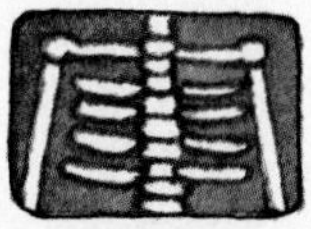

Y y

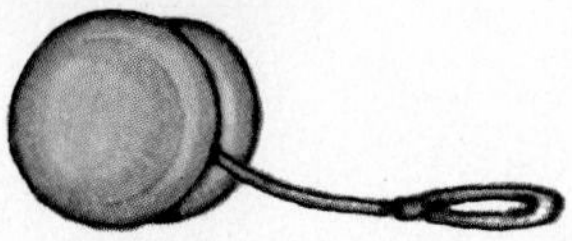

yard

yellow

yes

you'll

you're

your

yours

Z z

zoo

A

about My book is *about* animals.

above over. An airplane flew *above* us.

across on the other side of. Beth lives *across* the street.

add to put things together. If you *add* 2 and 3, you get 5. **added, adding**

after 5 comes *after* 4. We played *after* lunch.

again once more. Tell me that joke *again*.

against Put your bat *against* the wall.

ago at an earlier time. The game began an hour *ago*.

agree to think the same thing as someone else. I *agree* with Jan. **agreed, agreeing**

ahead before or in front of. Kim is *ahead* of Brad in the race.

aim to pick a spot to throw at. *Aim* at the middle of the target. **aimed, aiming**

airplane a machine that flies. People ride in it. An *airplane* flew above us. **airplanes**

alike the same. The twin brothers look *alike*.

alive able to eat and grow. Plants need water to stay *alive*.

alone without anyone else. Pat walked home *alone*.

along next to or with. Flowers grew *along* the path. May I go *along*?

any I don't have *any* paper.

anybody anyone. Jane didn't see *anybody* she knew.

anything Don likes *anything* made of chocolate.

apart not together. Keep the dogs *apart*.

apiece one for each person. We had one hamburger *apiece*.

April the fourth month of the year.

aren't the contraction for **are not**. They *aren't* ready yet.

arithmetic the use of numbers to solve a problem. We learned to add in *arithmetic* class.

around The puppy ran *around* the yard.

art when you make something to look at. In *art* class, we use paint, crayons, and clay.

as Bob is *as* tall *as* Jill.

asleep not awake. Terri fell *asleep* because she was tired.

August the eighth month of the year.

awake not asleep. I was *awake* by 7:00 this morning.

away   The squirrel ran *away* from us. Let's put *away* our books.

awhile   some time. I can stay for *awhile*.

B

back   behind the front. We sat in the *back* seat.

bake   to cook in an oven. *Bake* the cookies for ten minutes.   **baked, baking**

balloon   a toy made of thin rubber that you blow up.   **balloons**

bang   a loud noise. We could hear the *bang* of the drum.

barn   a building on a farm. The cows are in the *barn*.   **barns**

baseball   a game played with a ball and a bat. We need nine players for a *baseball* game.

bath   washing yourself in a tub of water. Ben takes a *bath* every night.   **baths**

beach   land next to water. This sandy *beach* is a good place to swim. **beaches**

bead   a small round object. It is used to make jewelry. This blue *bead* fell off Lisa's necklace.   **beads**

bean   a kind of vegetable. Sam ate only one green *bean*.   **beans**

beat   to hit something. Todd *beat* the drum as he marched.   **beating**

became   a form of **become**. She *became* a movie star.

because   a word used to tell why. Dan fell asleep *because* he was tired.

become   turn into. Ted wants to *become* a pilot someday.   **became, becoming**

bedtime   the time that you go to sleep. My *bedtime* is eight o'clock.

bee   an insect that can fly. A *bee* lives in a hive and makes honey.   **bees**

before   I wash my hands *before* I eat.

began   a form of **begin**. The show *began* an hour ago.

begin   to start. I should *begin* my homework now.   **began, beginning**

begun   a form of **begin**. It has *begun* to rain.

behave   to do the right thing. We must *behave* in school.   **behaved, behaving**

behind   in back of. Sean sat *behind* me on the bus.

believe   to think something is true. I *believe* Meg's story.   **believed, believing**

bell   something that rings. Our teacher rings a *bell* at noon.   **bells**

belong   owned by. These books *belong* to Jeff.   **belonged, belonging**

below   under. Hang the picture *below* the clock.

beneath   under. We sat *beneath* the oak tree.

beside   next to. Teri sat *beside* me on the bus.

best   Carl is the *best* speller in the class.

better   Kim feels *better* today.

between in the middle. Tim sat *between* Liz and Carlos.

beware be careful. *Beware* of that big dog.

beyond on the other side of. The cabin is *beyond* those trees.

bike a thing with wheels that you ride. **Bike** can also mean to ride a bike. Let's *bike* to the park. **biked, biking**

bird an animal that has feathers and two wings. Most birds can fly. **birds**

birthday the day you were born. **birthdays**

bite to put your teeth into something. Cats *bite* when they play. **bit, biting**

black a color. The sky looks *black* at night. **blacker, blackest**

block a hard piece of material. Adam carried a *block* of wood. **blocks**

blossom a flower on a plant or tree. **blossoms**

blow to make air come out of your mouth. Did Kara *blow* out her candles? **blew, blowing**

blue a color. The sky is *blue* today. **bluer, bluest**

book A book has pages with writing and pictures. She is reading the *book*. **books**

bookcase a set of shelves for books. **bookcases**

boot something you wear on your foot to keep it warm. **boots**

booth a small place for sitting or standing. You can call from that phone *booth*. **booths**

borrow to use something and then return it to its owner. You may *borrow* my red pen. **borrowed, borrowing**

both two together. Todd lost *both* of his mittens.

bottom the lowest part. Gail slid to the *bottom* of the hill.

bow[1] something you make when you tie a string or ribbon. Mom tied a pretty *bow* on the gift. **bows**

bow[2] to bend over a little. You must *bow* when you meet the King. **bowed, bowing**

bowl a deep, round dish. Ellie wants a *bowl* of soup. **bowls**

brain the part of your body that is inside your head. You use your brain to think and learn. **brains**

breakfast the meal you eat in the morning. **breakfasts**

bring to carry something with you. Did you *bring* your ball and bat? **brought, bringing**

broke a form of **break**. The cup *broke* when I dropped it.

brook a small river or stream. **brooks**

broom a brush with a long handle. It is used for sweeping. **brooms**

brown a color. Erin has *brown* hair. **browner, brownest**

bump a knock against something. Don't *bump* into the table. **bumped, bumping**

bunch many. Grapes grow in a *bunch*. **bunches**

button a small, round object that keeps clothing closed. **buttons**

buzz a sound. Bees *buzz* around the flowers. **buzzed, buzzing**

by near or next to. You may sit *by* me.

C

call to shout someone's name. **called, calling**

came a form of **come**. My dog *came* to school with me.

can't the contraction for **can not**. Dee *can't* find her hat.

car a machine that you ride in. **cars**

card a greeting that you send. We sent Nora a birthday *card*. **cards**

carpet something that covers the floor. The *carpet* in my room is green. **carpets**

chain a set of rings joined together. Bert locks his bike with a *chain*. **chains**

chair something you sit on. We need a *chair* for this desk. **chairs**

chance a turn to do something. Jan wants a *chance* to hold the kitten. **chances**

chat to talk for a little while. Barbara and Jill *chat* every day. **chatted, chatting**

check to look at carefully. Dentists *check* our teeth. **checked, checking**

cheek part of your face. Grandmother kissed me on the *cheek*. **cheeks**

cheer to shout in a happy voice. Let's *cheer* for our team. **cheered, cheering**

cheese a food made from milk. Kevin ate a ham and *cheese* sandwich. **cheeses**

chest part of the body below the neck. Your *chest* moves when you breathe. **chests**

chew to grind food with your teeth. *Chew* your food well before you swallow it. **chewed, chewing**

child a young girl or boy. Every *child* must go to school. **children**

chin the part of the face below the mouth. Darcy hit her *chin* on the bar. **chins**

chip a small piece of something. The beaver chewed a wood *chip*. **chips**

chirp a sound made by a bird. The birds *chirp* every morning. **chirped, chirping**

choose to pick. We *choose* Meg to be our leader. **chose, choosing**

chop to cut. Mr. Edwards must *chop* down that tree. **chopped, chopping**

church a place where people pray. Our family went to *church* on Sunday. **churches**

circle a round shape. Draw a *circle* around the number. **circles**

circus a show with animals and clowns. Dad took us to the *circus* last year. **circuses**

clay soft material that can be made into different shapes. We worked with *clay* in art class.

cling to hold tightly. Babies *cling* to their mothers. **clung, clinging**

close   to shut. *Close* the windows if it rains.   **closed, closing**

cold   not warm. I was *cold* without my sweater.   **colder, coldest**

cook   to heat food. Paul will *cook* the corn.   **cooked, cooking**

cookie   a small cake. Kyle ate a chocolate *cookie*.   **cookies**

cost   how much you must pay. The *cost* of these boots is fifteen dollars.

costume   something you dress up in. Jim wore a clown *costume*.   **costumes**

cow   an animal that gives milk.   **cows**

crack   a small opening. The rain came in through a *crack*.   **cracks**

cream   the thick part of milk. I poured *cream* on my cereal.

creep   to move quietly. We can *creep* by the sleeping baby.   **crept, creeping**

crow   a black bird. A *crow* flew over the cornfield.   **crows**

crowd   to put too many people or things in one place. Too many people will *crowd* the room.   **crowded, crowding**

crown   what kings and queens wear on their heads. The king wore a golden *crown*.   **crowns**

crunch   a noisy sound. Leaves *crunch* under my feet when I walk.   **crunched, crunching**

cry   to weep or sob. The sad movie made me *cry*.   **cried, crying**

cuff   the bottom of a long sleeve or pant leg.   **cuffs**

D

dash   to move quickly. I will *dash* home in the rain.   **dashed, dashing**

date   the month and the number of the day. Today's *date* is April 10.   **dates**

December   the twelfth month of the year.

deep   far down. The water is too *deep* here.   **deeper, deepest**

didn't   the contraction for **did not**. It *didn't* snow last night.

dirt   soil, mud, and dust.

dirty   not clean. Don't wear those *dirty* jeans.   **dirtier, dirtiest**

dive   to go into water head first. Scott can *dive* into the pool.   **dove, diving**

doghouse   a small house for a dog.   **doghouses**

doll   a toy that looks like a person.   **dolls**

doorbell   a bell you ring at a door. We rang the *doorbell*, but no one answered.   **doorbells**

down   lower. Put the book *down*. Patsy fell *down* and hurt her knee.

downhill   the direction from the top of a hill to the bottom. The ball rolled *downhill*.

dream   a thought or idea you have while sleeping. Pete had a *dream* about a spaceship.   **dreams**

duck   a bird that swims. It has webbed feet.   **ducks**

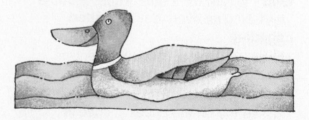

dull   not sharp. My scissors are too *dull*.   **duller, dullest**

E

each   every one. The cat washed *each* of her kittens.

east   a direction. Our house is *east* of Maple Street.

eat   to chew and swallow food. We *eat* lunch at noon.   **ate, eating**

egg   a shell that holds a baby bird until it hatches. A robin's *egg* has a blue shell.

eight   the number 8.

eighteen   the number 18.

eighth   number 8 in order.

eighty   the number 80.

eighty-one   the number 81.

elbow   where the arm bends. I bumped my *elbow* on the table.   **elbows**

eleven   the number 11.

eleventh   number 11 in order.

F

far   not close. Ted moved *far* away.

farm   a piece of land used to grow crops and raise animals. We grow corn on our *farm*.   **farms**

fast   moves quickly. Jamie is a *fast* runner.   **faster, fastest**

feast   a large, special meal. We had a *feast* on Thanksgiving.   **feasts**

February   the second month of the year. Valentine's Day is *February* 14.

feel   to touch something.   **felt, feeling**

feet   the plural of **foot**. My *feet* are tired from so much walking.

few   not very many. Katherine only had a *few* cents.   **fewer, fewest**

fifteen   the number 15.

fifth   number 5 in order.

fifty   the number 50.

fifty-five   the number 55.

finish   to end or be done. Please *finish* your work.   **finished, finishing**

fir   a tree that stays green all year.

firm   very strong. Bill has a *firm* handshake.

first   before everything else. The *first* person in line is the leader.

fish   an animal that lives in water.   **fish**

five   the number 5.

food   what people and animals eat.   **foods**

fool   to trick someone. My costume will *fool* the other children.   **fooled, fooling**

foot   the part of the body at the end of the leg. Craig can stand on one *foot*.   **feet**

football   a game played by two teams. Players kick, pass, and run with a ball.

forest   land covered with trees. Deer live in the *forest*.   **forests**

forty-four   the number 44.

four   the number 4.

fourteen   the number 14.

fourth   number 4 in order.

free   not costing anything. Balloons are *free* at the circus.

fresh   new. This store sells only *fresh* fruit.   **fresher, freshest**

Friday   a day of the week. It comes after Thursday.   **Fridays**

frown   to make a sad face. I *frown* when I am sad.   **frowned, frowning**

G

gate   the part of a fence that opens and closes. The horse ran through the open *gate*.   **gates**

gather   to collect or bring together. Let's *gather* the acorns from this tree.   **gathered, gathering**

gave   a form of **give**. Ann *gave* me her book yesterday.

girl   a female child.   **girls**

give   to let someone have something. I'll *give* you this book tomorrow.   **gave, giving**

good   fine or not bad. We played a *good* game.

goodbye   something you say when you are leaving. We said *goodbye* to Uncle Jay.

gown   a long dress. The queen wore a velvet *gown*.   **gowns**

grade   one year of school. Kelly is in second *grade*.   **grades**

grass   a thick green plant that covers the ground in many places. We sat on the *grass* and had a picnic.

gray   a color made by mixing black and white.   **grayer, grayest**

green   a color. We played on the soft, *green* grass.   **greener, greenest**

greet   to say hello. I *greet* my friends when I see them.   **greeted, greeting**

grill   something used to cook foods outside. We cooked hot dogs on the *grill*.   **grills**

grow   to get bigger. When I *grow*, this coat will fit.   **grew, growing**

H

hall   a long, narrow place in a building.   **halls**

Halloween   a holiday that comes on October 31. We dress in costumes on *Halloween*.

hammer   a tool used to pound nails.   **hammers**

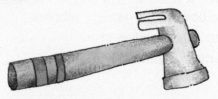

hang   to put something on a hook. *Hang* up your coat.   **hung, hanging**

hard   not soft. Clay gets *hard* when it dries.   **harder, hardest**

harm   to hurt. An unfriendly dog might *harm* you.   **harmed, harming**

has   Kristen *has* a green jacket. Brian *has* the ball.

hay   dried grass. Some farm animals eat *hay*.

heat   to make something hot. *Heat* the soup in this pan.   **heated, heating**

he'd   the contraction for **he had**. *He'd* already seen the movie.

heel   part of the foot. It is on the bottom near the ankle.   **heels**

he'll the contraction for **he will**. *He'll* be here soon.

hello something you say when you greet someone.

help to do something for someone. I'll *help* you carry those bags. **helped, helping**

her Beth combed *her* hair.

hers belonging to her. I wore my boots and Erin wore *hers*.

herself her alone. Lisa fixed the bicycle *herself*.

he's the contraction for **he is**. *He's* my best friend.

hide to go where you can't be found. We can *hide* under the porch. **hid, hiding**

him Steve hid in the attic, but we found *him*.

his belonging to him. Dave finished *his* work.

homesick what you feel when you want to go home. Jeanie was *homesick* at camp.

hood the part of a jacket or coat that covers your head. My coat has a *hood*. **hoods**

hoof the foot of a horse. **hooves**

hook a place on a wall to hang things. **hooks**

hope to want. I *hope* I get a new bike. **hoped, hoping**

how *How* do you feel? I'll show you *how* to play the game.

however We lost the game. *However*, we played well.

howl a loud sound made by some animals. Dogs *howl* when they are hungry. **howled, howling**

I

I'll the contraction for **I will**. *I'll* see you later.

I'm the contraction for **I am**. *I'm* seven years old.

I've the contraction for **I have**. *I've* seen that movie.

if We will swim *if* it is warm.

into Todd and Rita climbed *into* the car.

isn't the contraction for **is not**. This *isn't* my book.

it Nan wrote a poem and read *it* to the class.

it's the contraction for **it is**. *It's* Dana's birthday today.

its belonging to it. The bird broke *its* wing.

itself The squirrel can find food *itself*.

J

January the first month of the year.

jelly a sweet food made from fruit. Mom spread *jelly* on the bread. **jellies**

job work that must be done. It is my *job* to sweep the garage. **jobs**

joke a funny story. **Joke** also means to be funny. The clowns *joke* with each other. **joked, joking**

July the seventh month of the year. Our band marched in the 4th of *July* parade.

jump   to go up into the air. Can you *jump* over those bushes?   **jumped, jumping**

June   the sixth month of the year.

just   only. We can have *just* one cookie each.

K

kick   to hit something with your foot. Patsy can *kick* the ball far.   **kicked, kicking**

king   a man who rules a country. The *king* waved to the crowd.

kitten   a young cat. The mother cat washed her *kitten*.   **kittens**

L

laid   a form of **lay**. Pat *laid* the book on the table.

land   to touch the ground. The airplane will *land* soon.   **landed, landing**

large   very big. Elephants are *large* animals.   **larger, largest**

last   at the very end. *Z* is the *last* letter of the alphabet.

late   not on time. We'll be *late* if we don't hurry.   **later, latest**

lay   to put down. *Lay* your coats on the bed.   **laid, laying**

least   less than the rest. Beth found the *least* shells.

leave   to go away. I *leave* for school at nine o'clock.   **left, leaving**

less   not as much. Sandy weighs *less* than I do.

letter   *A* is the first *letter* of the alphabet.   **letters**

lettuce   a leafy green vegetable. Dad put *lettuce* on my sandwich.

like   to think something is good. I *like* this book about dinosaurs.   **liked, liking**

list   many things that are written down. Marty made a shopping *list*.   **lists**

long   not short. The giraffe has a *long* neck.   **longer, longest**

look   to see. *Look* at my new bike.   **looked, looking**

loose   not tight. These skates are *loose*.   **looser, loosest**

lost   missing. I found my *lost* mitten.

low   near the ground. I can reach the *low* branches of the tree.   **lower, lowest**

lunch   the meal you eat in the middle of the day.   **lunches**

M

made   a form of **make**. Yesterday we *made* a snowman.

mail   letters and packages brought by the post office. I got a letter in the *mail*.

main   important. Jessie got a *main* part in the play.

make   I *make* popcorn every Saturday night.   **made, making**

manner   the way you do things. Todd greets people in a polite *manner*.

many   a lot of something. The winning team had *many* good players.

March   the third month of the year.

mark   a spot. The water made a *mark* on my shorts.   **marks**

market   a place where food is sold. We buy meat at this *market*.   **markets**

math   the short form of the word **mathematics**. It is the study of numbers. Gina did her *math* homework.

matter   What's the *matter* with your arm? It doesn't *matter* if we lose.

May   the fifth month of the year.

may   to have permission. Dad says I *may* see that movie.

meal   breakfast, lunch or dinner. We helped prepare a special holiday *meal*.

mean   not nice. That was a *mean* thing to say.   **meaner, meanest**

meat   food we get from animals. We had *meat* for dinner.   **meats**

meet   to get to know a person. I'd like to *meet* the new girl.   **met, meeting**

mine   belonging to me. The blue jacket is *mine*.

miss   to wish you were with someone. I *miss* my brother when he goes to camp. **missed, missing**

mitten   a piece of clothing worn on the hand to keep it warm.   **mittens**

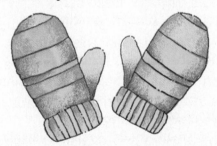

mix   to put all together. *Mix* the butter and sugar in this bowl.   **mixed, mixing**

Monday   a day of the week. *Monday* comes after Sunday.   **Mondays**

moon   We saw a full *moon* in the sky last night.   **moons**

moose   a large animal with big antlers.   **moose**

most   the greatest amount. Eric collected the *most* money.

much   How *much* do you weigh? I ate too *much* candy.

must   to have to do something. I *must* finish my homework.

my   *My* bike belongs to me. Have you seen *my* bat?

myself   the same as me. I can lift the box *myself*.

N

nail   a thin piece of metal that is pointed at one end. You use it to put things together.   **nails**

name   the word by which something is called. **Name** also means to choose this type of word. Let's *name* the gray kitten Smokey.   **named, naming**

narrow   thin or not wide. I walked behind Sally on the *narrow* path. **narrower, narrowest**

neck   the part of the body between the shoulders and the head. Karla tied a scarf around her *neck*.   **necks**

need   must have. I'll *need* my umbrella on this rainy day.   **needed, needing**

new   not used before. Mom's *new* car is clean and shiny.   **newer, newest**

next   right after. Paul is *next* in line.

nickel   a coin worth five cents. The pencil costs a *nickel*.   **nickels**

nine   the number 9.

nineteen   the number 19.

ninety-two   the number 92.

ninth   number 9 in order.

noon   twelve o'clock in the afternoon. At *noon*, we eat lunch.

not   I do *not* like snakes. His name is Josh, *not* John.

note   a very short letter. Berta wrote a thank-you *note* to Maria. **notes**

nothing   There was *nothing* on the table.

November   the eleventh month of the year. We celebrate Thanksgiving in *November*.

now   right away. *Now* I'll watch TV. Mom needs the eggs *now*.

O

October   the tenth month of the year. Halloween is *October* 31.

odd   strange. *Odd* little creatures ran from the spaceship. **odder, oddest**

off   not on. The lamp is *off*.

old   not new. My *old* shoes are too small for me. **older, oldest**

one   the number 1.

only   Molly is the *only* girl in her family.

other   Where is my *other* mitten? Bob has *other* plans for Saturday.

our   *Our* teacher drew the map. That's *our* bus.

ours   belonging to us. The green car is *ours*.

ourselves   Dad and I made the cake *ourselves*.

owl   a bird with a round head, large eyes, and thick feathers. An owl stays awake at night. **owls**

own   to have. We *own* this house. **owner**

P

paid   a form of **pay**. Mona *paid* one dollar for the book.

paint   colored liquid that changes the color of something. Tom brushed white *paint* on the old fence. **paints**

pancake   a round, flat breakfast food. **pancakes**

parade   a march with bands, floats, animals, and clowns. Our band marched in the 4th of July *parade*. **parades**

park   an outdoor place where people go to play or rest. **parks**

part   a piece of something. One *part* of this puzzle is missing. **parts**

partner   someone you do something with. Kathie is my tennis *partner*. **partners**

past   the time that has gone by. I made new friends this *past* year.

paste   to use glue to hold things together. I'll *paste* these cards in my scrapbook. **pasted, pasting**

path   a place to walk. This *path* goes through the woods. **paths**

pattern   colors and shapes on something. Tim's scarf has a green and white *pattern*. **patterns**

peas   a small, round, green vegetable that grows in pods. This vegetable soup has carrots and *peas* in it.

pick   to choose. I *pick* Sharon for our team. **picked, picking**

pie   a baked crust that is filled with fruit. We had cherry *pie* for dessert. **pies**

pillow   a cloth case filled with foam or feathers. Cindy put her head on her *pillow* and went to sleep.   **pillows**

pinch   to squeeze something between two fingers. Dad likes to *pinch* me on my cheek.

plain   not fancy. Sarah wore a *plain* blue dress.   **plainer, plainest**

plow   to make soil ready for seeds. Farmers *plow* the land before they plant seeds.   **plowed, plowing**

plus   and or also. Two *plus* three is five. There will be five of us, *plus* the dog.

pocket   an opening in clothing to put things in. I keep my keys in my coat *pocket*.   **pockets**

polish   to rub something until it shines. Ted will wash and *polish* your car.   **polished, polishing**

pool   a place built for swimming. Teri can swim across the *pool*.   **pools**

powder   dry, ground up matter. Dad put some *powder* on the baby.   **powders**

praise   good things said about someone. Dogs need *praise* when they behave well.

pretty   nice to look at. The pink roses in the garden look *pretty*.   **prettier, prettiest**

pry   to try to force open. We'll have to *pry* the lid off the jelly jar.   **pried, prying**

purr   a low sound that cats make. **purred, purring**

push   to use your weight to move something. We must *push* the car home. **pushed, pushing**

Q

quack   the sound a duck makes. **quacks**

queen   a woman ruler. The *queen* rode to the palace.   **queens**

R

rabbit   an animal with long ears and a fluffy tail.   **rabbits**

race   to try to get somewhere first. Let's *race* to the corner.   **raced, racing**

rain   drops of water that fall from the sky. The dry garden needs *rain*.

rainbow   a band of colors that appears in the sky after it rains.   **rainbows**

raindrop   a drop of rain. A *raindrop* landed on my nose.   **raindrops**

rake   We *rake* the leaves and put them in bags.   **raked, raking**

rang   a form of **ring**. The doorbell *rang* three times.

reach   to get something with your hand. Are you tall enough to *reach* the top shelf? **reached, reaching**

ready   prepared. I'm *ready* for the spelling test.

red   a color. A *red* light means stop. **redder, reddest**

rest   to stop and relax for a while. We can *rest* on this bench.   **rested, resting**

ring   to make a sound like a bell. Did you hear the telephone *ring*?   **rang, ringing**

rocket   a ship that travels through space.   **rockets**

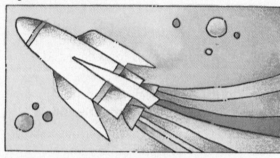

room   part of a house or building. My *room* is upstairs.   **rooms**

rope   a long cord used to tie things. **Rope** also means to throw a rope around something. The cowboy can *rope* a cow as he rides his horse.   **roped, roping**

row   to move a boat with oars. Let's *row* the boat back to shore.   **rowed, rowing**

rubber   soft, firm material that bounces. This ball is made of *rubber.*

rule   to act as the leader of a country. The king and queen *rule* their country.   **ruled, ruling**

run   to move as fast as you can. Baseball players must *run* fast.   **ran, running**

rush   to hurry. Let's *rush* home before it rains.   **rushed, rushing**

S

sail   a piece of cloth attached to a boat. It catches the wind and makes the boat go.   **sails**

sang   a form of **sing**. Yesterday we *sang* a new song.

Saturday   a day of the week. *Saturday* comes after Friday.

scatter   to throw things around. Let's *scatter* crumbs for the birds.   **scattered, scattering**

school   a place you go to learn. **schools**

screen   a covering for a window. It is made of wire.   **screens**

sea   a large body of salt water. Mr. Turner likes to fish in the *sea.*   **seas**

seal   an animal that lives in the water. A *seal* likes to swim.   **seals**

season   a time of the year. Winter is my favorite *season.*   **seasons**

seat   a place to sit. Lynn took a *seat* in the front row.   **seats**

second   number 2 in order. February is the *second* month of the year.

seed   part of a plant. A new plant grows from a *seed.*   **seeds**

seem   Cars *seem* tiny from an airplane. **seemed, seeming**

September   the ninth month of the year.

seven   the number 7.

seventeen   the number 17.

seventh   number 7 in order. Susan is in *seventh* grade.

seventy   the number 70.

shadow   a dark shape that something makes when it is in the light. My *shadow* seems to follow me.   **shadows**

shake   to move something up and down. *Shake* the can of paint before you use it.   **shook, shaking**

shape the form of something. Her face has an oval *shape*. **shapes**

sharp very pointed. The cat has *sharp* claws. **sharper, sharpest**

she a word used in place of a girl's name. I called Jan, but *she* wasn't home.

sheet a covering for the mattress of a bed. **sheets**

she'll the contraction for **she will**. Mom said *she'll* help us make our costumes.

shirt a piece of clothing worn on the top part of the body. His *shirt* is blue. **shirts**

shoe a piece of clothing worn on the foot. **shoes**

shook a form of **shake**. The puppy *shook* his tail.

shop a small store. This *shop* sells hats. **shops**

shore the land near the sea. We found pretty shells along the *shore*. **shores**

short not very tall. Becky is *short* for her age. **shorter, shortest**

shove to push. Don't push and *shove* in line. **shoved, shoving**

shovel a tool with a long handle and a flat part. It is used for digging. **shovels**

show to let others see something. Let me *show* you a new magic trick. **showed, showing**

shower water spraying down. Kate took a *shower* before she got dressed. **showers**

shy afraid of new people. Karen was too *shy* to speak in class. **shyer, shyest**

side one part of something. Our team plays on this *side* of the field. **sides**

sing to use your voice to make music. Let's *sing* "Happy Birthday" to Michelle. **sang, singing**

sir a word you use to show respect for a man. *Sir*, will you help me?

six the number 6.

sixth number 6 in order. My brother is in *sixth* grade.

sixty the number 60.

skirt a piece of clothing that is worn around the waist. Pat wore a red *skirt*. **skirts**

sky the air high above us. The *sky* looks cloudy today. **skies**

slow taking a long time. We waited for the *slow* train to pass. **slower, slowest**

sly tricky. The *sly* fox tricked the Gingerbread Man. **slier, sliest**

smell what you do with your nose. I *smell* cookies baking. **smelled, smelling**

snail a small animal that lives in water. It moves very slowly. **snails**

snow frozen rain. Snow also means frozen rain falling. It may *snow* tonight if it gets colder. **snowed, snowing**

snowball a ball made from snow. **snowballs**

snowman a statue made of snow. The children built a *snowman* in the park. **snowmen**

sock a piece of clothing worn under the shoe. Lisa wore long yellow *socks*. **socks**

something There is *something* in this box for you. I have *something* to tell you.

song music and words that you sing. We learned a *song* about spring. **songs**

soon in a short time. The pizza will be done *soon*. **sooner, soonest**

speak to talk. I'll *speak* to Uncle Dave about the problem. **spoke, speaking**

speed to go very fast. I can *speed* down this hill on my skateboard. **sped, speeding**

spill to let something fall out. Don't *spill* the paint. **spilled, spilling**

spinach a leafy green vegetable. Put the *spinach* in the salad.

splash to throw water. The children *splash* each other in the pool. **splashed, splashing**

spoke a form of **speak**. Dad *spoke* to Jean about her homework.

spoon a tool you use for eating. You eat soup with a *spoon*. **spoons**

spring the season between March 21 and June 21. New plants grow in the *spring*. **springs**

squirm to twist and turn your body. Please don't *squirm* in your seat. **squirmed, squirming**

squirt to spray. Please don't *squirt* me with your water gun! **squirted, squirting**

stand to be on your feet. We had to *stand* in line. **stood, standing**

start to begin. The game will *start* at one o'clock. **started, starting**

stick a thin piece of wood. **sticks**

sting Bees *sting* when they bite you. **stung, stinging**

stir to mix. *Stir* the cake batter. **stirred, stirring**

stood a form of **stand**. The police officer *stood* on the corner.

stool a three or four-legged seat without a back. Kris stood on a *stool* to reach the shelf. **stools**

storybook a book with many stories. **storybooks**

street a road in a city or town. Turn right on this *street*. **streets**

string strong, thin material used to tie things. **strings**

strong powerful. The *strong* wind shook the house. **stronger, strongest**

stuff a word for all sorts of things. Put this *stuff* away.

such Meg is *such* a friendly girl.

sudden without warning. The boxer made a *sudden* move.

Sunday a day of the week. We go to church on *Sunday*. **Sundays**

sunshine the warmth and light of the sun. These plants need plenty of *sunshine*.

sweet tasting like sugar. This fudge is very *sweet*. **sweeter, sweetest**

swell to get bigger. Did your ankle *swell* when you broke it? **swelled, swelling**

swing a seat on ropes or chains that moves back and forth. **swings**

T

tail part of an animal. The kitten chases her own *tail*. **tails**

tall long and far from the ground. Mom's office is in that *tall* building. **taller, tallest**

target something you aim at. Scott hit the *target* and won the game. **targets**

team a group working or playing together. Our baseball *team* is ready for the game. **teams**

ten the number 10.

tenth number 10 in order. October is the *tenth* month of the year.

test questions to find out how much you know. Patty studied for the spelling *test*. **tests**

than My dog is older *than* yours. This book is thicker *than* that one.

thank to tell someone that you like what that person did for you. I *thank* my friends for their gifts. **thanked, thanking**

that Do you want this book or *that* one? *That* was a good movie.

that's the contraction for **that is**. *That's* my little brother.

their *Their* house is across the street. This is *their* car.

theirs belonging to them. This house is ours, and that one is *theirs*.

them The boys asked us to play with *them*.

there Put the box over *there*.

these *These* socks are too small.

thick big around. The *thick* book has many pages. **thicker, thickest**

thing an object. Is there one *thing* you want for your birthday? **things**

think to use your brain. I'll *think* about the question. **thought, thinking**

third number 3 in order. March is the *third* month of the year.

thirsty needing a drink. The *thirsty* boy drank two glasses of water.

thirteen the number 13.

thirty the number 30.

thirty-three the number 33.

this *This* is my brother, José. I like *this* color best.

those These cards are his and *those* are mine.

three the number 3.

throw to send through the air. *Throw* the ball to Gary. **threw, throwing**

Thursday a day of the week. **Thursdays**

ticket a piece of paper you need to get into a movie, play, or game. Tina bought a *ticket* for the game. **tickets**

time to see how long something takes. Dad will *time* the race. **timed, timing**

today this day. *Today* is Kevin's birthday.

together with another person. Sue and Al built the treehouse *together*.

tomorrow the day after today. Today is Monday. *Tomorrow* will be Tuesday.

too also. Can Tracey come, *too*?

took a form of **take**. Lisa *took* the kitten home.

tooth the white things in your mouth used for chewing and biting. **teeth**

towel a cloth used to dry something. Dry your hands with the *towel*. **towels**

town a small city. **towns**

trail a narrow road or path. We rode our bikes on a *trail* through the park. **trails**

train cars that are joined together and run on tracks. Dad rides the *train* to work each day. **trains**

tree   a tall plant with branches, leaves, and a trunk.   **trees**

trick   to fool. We *trick* each other on Halloween.   **tricked, tricking**

Tuesday   a day of the week.   **Tuesdays**

twelfth   number 12 in order. December is the *twelfth* month of the year.

twelve   the number 12.

twenty   the number 20.

twenty-five   the number 25.

twenty-two   the number 22.

twice   two times. Bill called me *twice.*

twirl   to turn around quickly. Amy can *twirl* a baton.   **twirled, twirling**

two   the number 2.

U

up   toward the ceiling or sky. Mom lifted the baby *up.*

upon   on. Gary put the silly hat *upon* my head.

us   the same as **we.** Dad helped *us* make the cake.

use   to do something with an object. I'll *use* this crayon to color the picture. **used, using**

V

very   A giant is *very* tall. I like chocolate ice cream *very* much.

vote   to say you are for or against something. I will *vote* for Sheri.   **voted, voting**

vowel   any of the letters **a, e, i, o,** or **u.** **vowels**

W

wait   to stay somewhere. Let's *wait* here for the bus.   **waited, waiting**

wall   one side of a room or building. Jessie hung the picture on the *wall.* **walls**

want   to wish for. Paula and her sister *want* a puppy.   **wanted, wanting**

wash   to use water to make something clean. We *wash* our hands before lunch.   **washed, washing**

way   how you get somewhere. We go this *way* to school.   **ways**

weak   not strong. Joe felt *weak* when he was sick.   **weaker, weakest**

Wednesday   a day of the week. **Wednesdays**

week   seven days. We will be home in a *week.*   **weeks**

we'll   the contraction for **we will.** *We'll* play indoors today.

well   If you did something well, you did a good job. Ted sang *well.*

went   Kristy *went* home with Sara. William *went* to the park.

west   a direction. California is *west* of Arizona.

we've   the contraction for **we have.** *We've* been looking for you.

whale   a very large animal that lives in the ocean.   **whales**

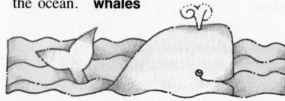

what   *What* is your name? I didn't hear *what* you said.

wheat   a crop that farmers grow. It is used to make flour.

wheel   a round object that turns and makes things go. Dad turned the steering *wheel* of the car.   **wheels**

when   *When* can you come? Sandra goes to bed *when* she gets tired.

where   *Where* is your house?

which   *Which* jacket is yours?

whiff   a smell of something. Ted got a *whiff* of the cookies.   **whiffs**

while   during. We ate popcorn *while* we watched the movie.

whimper   to cry softly. The baby may *whimper* for his mother.   **whimpered, whimpering**

whine   to cry and complain. Some children *whine* when they are tired. **whined, whining**

whip   an object used to hit something. The lion tamer held a *whip*.   **whips**

whiskers   the long hairs on each side of a cat's face.

whisper   to speak very softly. We *whisper* when the baby is sleeping. **whispered, whispering**

whistle   to blow a musical sound out of your lips. You sing the song and I'll *whistle* it.   **whistled, whistling**

white   a color. Snow is *white*.   **whiter, whitest**

why   *Why* are you sad? I know *why* Scott went home.

will   Ms. Martin *will* teach our class. *Will* you come with me?

window   a glass opening in a wall. We looked out the *window* and saw a robin. **windows**

wing   the part of a bird's or insect's body that helps it fly.   **wings**

with   I sat *with* Carrie on the bus.

without   A car won't go *without* gas.

wood   the material we get from trees. The table is made of *wood*.

woods   a place where many trees grow together. We went for a hike in the *woods*.

wool   something used to make cloth. It comes from sheep.

work   to do a job. Many people *work* at night.   **worked, working**

Y

yard   the land around a house. We raked the leaves in our *yard*.   **yards**

yellow   a color. Our school bus is *yellow*.   **yellower, yellowest**

yes   a word you say when you agree. *Yes*, I can come to your party.

you'll   the contraction for **you will**. *You'll* like this puppet show.

your   Is this *your* house? *Your* mother is calling you.

you're   the contraction for **you are**. *You're* my best friend.

yours   belonging to you. *Yours* is the best costume.

yourself   you alone. Can you finish the job *yourself*?

Z

zoo   a place where animals are kept for people to see. Our *zoo* has a new elephant.   **zoos**

Handwriting Practice

wh

why

what

when

where

sh

she

shop

fish

wash

th

think

them

bath

with

ch

chin

chair

child

each

much

ck

back

kick

neck

sock

ir

bird

skirt

firm

girl

circle

ow

elbow

grow

snow

throw

window

be

become

before

begin

behind

tt

letter

mitten

oo

ng

ai

ea

ed

ing

st

wh

sh

th

ch

ck

er

est

ir

ow

be

tt

Proofreading Practice

Lessons 1–4   Photo Captions

Proofreading Marks	
— Take something out.	I like ~~schoool~~. (school)
∧ Put something in.	I learn ∧ things. (many)
≡ Use a capital letter.	luis sits by me.
/ Use a lowercase letter.	He is my Friend.
⊙ Add a period.	We have fun ⊙

Dana has written captions for some photos of her art class. Mark the mistakes she made. Use the proofreading marks in the box. Then correct her errors as you make a clean copy of the captions on your own paper.

Here we are makeing clay pots.

The grae clay is very wet.

Our clay is baking in the oven

only one pot brok.

Some pots are as blue as the Sky.

Others as redd as roses.

Your Turn Draw pictures to show how to do something. Write sentences to go with your pictures. Try to use some long vowel words that end in silent **e** or some words with an **ing** ending. Then proofread your work.

Ari's class is learning about the jobs people do. Ari wrote about a cook. Mark the mistakes he made. Watch for misspelled words, words that should have capital letters, missing words, and missing end marks. Then correct his errors as you make a clean copy of his report on your own paper.

My dad is a Cook. Each

morning he choses what will make

that day. He cooks the food for a lon

time he uses many spices. He like

to sing as he works. My dad does

not need to read a book to make

gud food.

Your Turn Write about a job you would like to do. Use some words that are spelled with **oo** or some words that end in **ng**. Then proofread your work.

Juan had many chores. He made a list of the things he had to do. Then he shared the list with his parents. Mark the mistakes Juan made. Watch for misspelled words, mistakes with capital letters, and missing words and end marks. Then correct his errors as you make a clean copy of his list on your own paper.

Things I Must Do

1. Put away my trans.

2. Clean the green beens.

3. Go to the merket with Mom.

4. Paint a picture for Grandma

5. Male a get-well card to mrs Lee.

6. Meat Mark in the Park noon.

Your Turn Write a list of the things you must do today. Try to use some words that are spelled with **ai, ar, ee,** and **ea.** Then proofread your work.

Marta wrote a story about a boy who finds a magic chest. She wants to make it into a book. Mark the mistakes Marta made. Watch for misspelled words, words that do not belong, mistakes with capital letters, and missing end marks. Then correct Marta's errors as you make a clean copy of her story on your own paper.

Ben was on his way west. He

had walked far. He whanted to rest

Ben needed to eat. In some tall

grass lay a large paintid Chest.

Ben he smeld eggs, meat pies,

cheese, and beans. He look inside.

What a feast!

Your Turn Will Ben eat the food? Who might leave such a chest in the grass? Write what happens next. Try to use some words that end with double consonants and with the letters **st**. Then proofread your work. Watch for verbs that end in **ing** and **ed**.

Taro wrote a paragraph to describe his favorite place. Now he plans to share his ideas with his class. Mark the mistakes Taro made. Watch for misspelled words, mistakes with capital letters, and missing words and end marks. Then correct his errors as you make a clean copy of his paragraph on your own paper.

> We live by the Sea. I like to gathher
>
> shells on the beach. My family and I chat
>
> as we fish from the rocks. We splash near
>
> shore wile wales whine and dive at sea.
>
> This is why I like my home.

Your Turn Write a paragraph to describe your favorite place. Try to use some words that are spelled with **ch, sh, th,** and **wh.** Then proofread your work.

Here is a book report Alec wrote for his school newspaper. Mark the mistakes Alec made. Watch for misspelled words, mistakes with capital letters, and missing end marks. Then correct his errors as you make a clean copy of his book report on your own paper.

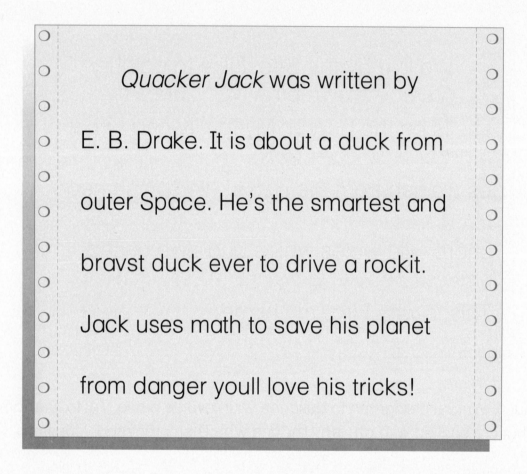

Quacker Jack was written by

E. B. Drake. It is about a duck from

outer Space. He's the smartest and

bravst duck ever to drive a rockit.

Jack uses math to save his planet

from danger youll love his tricks!

Your Turn Write about a book you have read. Try to use some contractions and words that end with **er** and **est**. Then proofread your work.

Rita wants her class to know about a special bird. Here is the paragraph she wrote. Mark the mistakes Rita made. Watch for misspelled words, wrong or missing words, words that should have capital letters, and missing end marks. Then correct Rita's errors as you make a clean copy of her paragraph on your own paper.

A small brown bird lives above my window. I awake to it's cheerful chirp. I bring it fresh water in a a little red bole. It bouws to show its thanks then it flies away abuve the tallest trees in our town.

Your Turn Write a paragraph that describes a person or an animal you find interesting. Use some words that are spelled with **ir**. Proofread your work. Pay special attention to words that are spelled with **ow**.

Carrie's aunt sent her some birthday presents. Carrie decided to send her aunt a thank-you letter. Mark the mistakes Carrie made. Watch for misspelled words, mistakes with capital letters, and missing words and end marks. Then correct Carrie's errors as you make a clean copy of her letter on your own paper.

May 10, 19—

Dear Aunt helena

Thank you for the birthday gifts

I've read the Storybook seven times.

The mitens are great becuze began

ice-skating today.

Love,

Carrie

Your Turn Imagine that you have received a special gift. Write a thank-you letter to tell the giver how much you like it. Use some compound words in your letter. Proofread your work. Watch for words with double consonants in the middle.